Streets of London

A Guide to the Five Streets Featured in the Thames Television Series

by

David Benedictus

with photographs by

Cressida Pemberton-Pigott

THAMES METHUEN
LONDON
1985

First published in November 1985
to accompany the Thames Television series
Programme Producer: Peter Denton
Programme Researcher: Alice Harper
Executive Producer: Diana Potter

Published by Thames Television International Ltd
149 Tottenham Court Road, London W1P 9LL

Distributed by Methuen (Associated Book Publishers)
11 New Fetter Lane, London EC4P 4EE

ISBN 0 423 01830 2

Cover concept by Rob Page
Book Design by Thames Television Publishing Department
Phototypset in Goudy Old Style by Stratatype, London NW1
Printed by Whitstable Litho, Whitstable, Kent

Contents

Introduction

Sometimes in the crowded Goodge Street Underground lifts I indulge my fantasy. I transport these anxious, tired, overwrought commuters to some coral island, and there they disport themselves, abandoning carrier bag and plastic mac, *Ms London* and briefcase on that outcrop of sea-washed rock, tearing off pin-stripe and two-piece for the boisterous delights of the reef and the glade, barbecued shark under the star-spangled sky, native nights of conch-music and warm thighs. Oh, how they would revel in it, these molish Londoners with their earth-worn complexions, how they would blossom and bud and flower under the equatorial sun! And then we jerk to a halt and the new gates crash open – how cruelly bright the light – and into the glitzy vulgarity of the Tottenham Court Road, fast foods and electronic component suppliers, betting shops and retailers of louvre doors, neon-lit offices in which clerks are driven mad by memos, and tin-pot dictators pace up and down their nylon carpets from advertising calendar to year-planner; oh Tottenham Court Road!

It's a haunted road too, for where Tottenham Court Road meets Oxford Street there used to be a large round stone, upon which the chanting boys of St Giles were whipped, those who deserved whipping and some perhaps who did not. And it was in Tottenham Court Road that Richard Brothers, alias 'The Prophet' once met the devil 'walking leisurely'.

But it was at Tottenham Court that Londoners feasted on cakes and ale in the seventeenth century and where girls, according to Ben Jonson, went to eat cream. For there used to be a very fine farm house near St Giles with seventy acres of 'extraordinary good pastures and meadows, with all conveniences proper for a cowman . . . and dung ready to lay in'.

I confess that with this casual mention of Tottenham Court Road, I am all agog to include that prosaic street amongst my five. But I must not. Delve into the history of London and it's like opening the treasure chest of a wrecked flag-ship; endlessly fascinating. Read Mayhew's master-piece, *London Labour and the London Poor,* published in 1851, and you enter a world inhabited by the young man who made a living out of swallowing snakes – 'You must cut the stinger out or he'll injure you. The tail is slippery, but you nip it with the nails like pinchers. If you was to let him go, he'd go right down; but most snakes will stop at two inches down the swallow, and then they bind like a ball in the mouth.' And by Messrs Tiffin and Son, Bug-Destroyers to Her Majesty and the Royal Family. And by the Doll's-Eye Maker who also manufactured human eyes: 'The generality of persons whom we serve take out their eyes when they go to bed, and sleep with them either under their pillow, or else in a tumbler of water on the toilet-table at their side. Most married ladies, however, never take their eyes out at all.' And a host of other eccentrics who scratched a living out of a city as savage and enchanted as Xanadu. Savage, if you read Blake and de Quincey and Dickens and Arthur Morrison. 'This hellish and all-devouring wen,' said Cobbett. 'This compound of fen-fog, chimney-smoke, smuts, and pulverized horse-dung,' said Southey. 'Gloomy, morose, huckstering, repulsive,' wrote Ali-Chim-Le, and Carlyle called London 'acrid putrescence'. Enchanted, though, to Dr Johnson, of course, and to Henry James and to Ford Madox Ford, and to me.

There is a passage in Benjamin Haydon's autobiography, written in 1805, which sums its enchantment up splendidly. Haydon, historical painter, perpetual bankrupt, madman and suicide is talking to John Fuseli, fantasist and keeper of the Royal Academy.

'Be Gode,' says Fuseli, who was born in Zurich, as he observes the pall of smoke overhanging London like a sublime canopy, 'it's like de smoke of de Israelites making bricks.' 'It is grander,' Haydon replies, 'for it is the smoke of a people who would have made the Egyptians make bricks for them.' 'Well done, John Bull,' says Fuseli. And Haydon remarks on how sometimes through the drifted clouds you may catch a glimpse of the great dome of St Paul's 'announcing at once civilisation and power'.

Savage, but not as savage as it used to be with its plagues and its pestilences, its cock-fighting and bear-baiting, and the Mohawks or Mohocks who terrorised the city, cutting off the hands and slitting the noses of those who caught their eye. Enchanted, but not as enchanted as it must – eventually – have seemed to Richard Whittington, Lord Mayor, nor to Venetia Stanley (1600–33) whose beauty caused the Duke of Dorset to pay her an annuity of five hundred pounds, and Sir Kenelm Digby to marry her. Her premature death was caused, some claimed, by her husband's dosing her with viper wine to preserve her beauty; it is generally agreed that after her death Digby never shaved again. It was Venetia of whom Ben Jonson wrote:

To one, she said, Do this, he did it; So
To another, Move; he went; to a third, Go,
He run; and all did strive with diligence
T'obey and serve her sweet Commandments.

I see none such in the lift at Goodge Street. And of savagery and enchantment, only occasional flickers. But then the fogs are not as thick as they used to be, and modern Mohocks put parking tickets on the windscreens of cars.

Five streets, they said they wanted, and it seemed as unrealistic as just ten commandments to live by, or a mere seven days of the week to create the world in. Five streets, they said, but evidently their minds were elsewhere, because how could I ignore Piccadilly, or the King's Road, or Bayswater Road, or the Edgware Road, or Regent Street, or the Embankment?

And already that is more than five. Which is not counting Fleet Street, that granite monument to ephemeral ideas, nor Bond Street ('I like to walk down Bond Street, thinking of all the things I don't want,' wrote Logan Pearsall Smith), nor the hopelessly respectable Baker Street, nor Primrose Hill fluttering with kites, nor Blackheath, haunted by ghastly highwaymen, nor . . .

But there is material here for a whole library of books, and decades of tramping through the savage enchantment of London. Only then shall I have earned my coral island, but I'm not at all sure that it won't seem a little, well, tame, when finally I get there. As Wilde pointed out with characteristic acerbity: 'Shakespeare wrote nothing but doggerel lampoon before he came to London and never penned a line after he left.'

1

Marylebone Road

The original by-pass

Then we abroad to Marrowbone, and there walked in the garden, the first time I ever was there, and a pretty place it is.

— *Samuel Pepys 1668*

The problem was traffic congestion. In the mid eighteenth century, as in the late twentieth. By 1755 things had become so hectic in Oxford Street that the graziers, salesmen and butchers petitioned Parliament for a by-pass. They would be driving their cattle to Smithfield when an ox, alarmed by one of the numerous carriages, would run amok, killing or wounding pedestrians, damaging the stock of the street traders, and terrifying everybody. And frequently market day would coincide with a hanging at Tyburn.

Now a Tyburn hanging was a matter for great decorum. Sessions would be held about eight times a year, after which some twenty malefactors would be sent to Tyburn. The criminals would process through the streets in carts, wearing their best clothes and with nosegays and white gloves. Usually the gloves would not be worn until the procession reached Tyburn for it lowered the tone if the gloves became grubby or besmirched. It has been computed that not less than 50,000 people were hanged at Tyburn between 1196 and 1783, from boys accused of stealing a few pence to Perkin Warbeck, William Wallace, and the Holy Maid of Kent, Elizabeth Barton, who was courageous enough to reproach Henry VIII for his licentious life. No fewer than 81 martyrs died at Tyburn, including the Blessed Oliver Plunket, and of these 81, 23 have been declared venerable.

As the Rev. P. Fletcher wrote, in *The Road to Tyburn:*

When we in motor buses ride
The Martyrs went to hurdles tied . . .
Tyburn to us is a sweet story
Tyburn to them was death and glory.

Left: Marylebone Road, looking east from the roof garden of Berkeley Court.

Most of the condemned men would be shaved and pomaded and looking pretty fine, with girls dressed in white, scattering flowers and oranges along the way, and friends ready by the gallows to pull on the legs or beat the breasts of their unfortunate intimates.

But the point I am labouring to make is that with Oxford Street crowded with shoppers and twenty hangings taking place, there was just no way that the drovers were going to get their stock to Smithfield without disasters along the way, and Parliament agreed in 1756 that something would have to be done. Another consideration for MPs was that in times of public danger when invasion was threatened by the French or the Dutch, a new road to the north of Oxford Street 'would form a complete line of circumvallation and his Majesty's Forces might, easily and expeditiously, march that way without the inconvenience of passing through the Cities of London and Westminster'.

I expect there was an outcry from the conservationists among the residents. As Pepys remarked, it was a pretty place, Marrowbone. But then, as now, there were those anxious to make a killing out of the splendid new business that the New Road (as it was called) would create. This is an advertisement, published four years after the Act of Parliament, for tea-rooms in Marylebone Gardens:

> Tarts of a twelvepenny size will be made every day from one to three o'clock . . . The almond cheesecakes will be always hot at one o'clock as usual; and the rich seed and plum cakes sent to any part of the town, at 2s 6d each. Coffee, tea and chocolate, at any time of the day, and fine Epping butter may also be had.

Nor were refreshments all the gardens had to offer. They were famous for their bowling-greens, their concerts and the nearby City of Oxford Tavern, where James Figg, champion prize-fighter, cudgeller and fencer, presided. 'You should go to Marylebone to learn valour,' runs a line in John Gay's *The Beggar's Opera*. 'These are the schools that have made so many brave men.'

I may be unintentionally misleading you. Pepys's reference to Marrowbone was just Pepys practising the demotic. There is no mention of Marrowbone or Marylebone in Domesday Book. The name Marylebone comes from the Church of 'St Mary on the bourne', the bourne being the Tyburn. St-Mary-by-the-brook, then, was the charming name of a charming village, with its own park which was used for hunting. According to Pevsner, no less a person than the Russian Ambassador hunted there in 1601, together with his entourage of Muscovites. There was even a manor house built in the reign of Henry VIII and pulled down in 1791 to make way for Devonshire Place.

Right: 'Westway can look quite astonishing. . .' (See overleaf.)

But the New Road was not just to be any old road. It was to be managed by the St Marylebone Turnpike Trust and tolls were to be collected, the money being used to maintain the road. Even more to the point the road was to be at least forty feet wide, with a further fifty feet either side of the road before houses could be erected. The effect would be 'to keep the road dry by having the benefit of the sun's rays and an open current and circulation of air'. Obviously with cows and sheep and poultry, the fine new road could easily become a quagmire.

Well, of course, in rather over two hundred years the grandiose and imaginative schemes of the Parliamentary Committee have been rather compromised. It was never anticipated that the Marylebone Road should start with a raised motorway extension and end with an underpass. But even these modern depredations have had some happy results. Since the sun sinks in the west, Westway can look quite astonishing at dusk on a hot summer's day as one looks up at it from the Marylebone Road. And driving east in the morning the phallus of the Post Office Tower, almost circumcised by Irish terrorists shortly after it was opened to the public, stands out like a minaret, while the Church of the Holy Trinity is silhouetted against the glass and concrete of Euston Tower, briefly – in 1969 – the tallest building in London.

It was shortly after the New Road was completed that the Brothers Adam conceived their grand design of Portland Place, 125 feet wide and, with the exception of Parliament Street, the broadest street in London. Tactfully the brothers named it after their landlord. Working for the Prince Regent thirty-two years later, John Nash designed a magnificent development for Regent's Park, part of which involved extending Port-land Place northwards with a fine circle of buildings (Regent's Circle) where it joined the New Road (later Marylebone Road). This circle would have been the largest circle of building in Europe. But Park Crescent and Park Square, with its whimsical Doric lodges, are all that were completed.

A few words about John Nash. The son of a Lambeth millwright, he was orphaned as a child and bankrupt as a young man. Nothing daunted, in the year of the French Revolution he married a woman who was not only much younger than himself, but also the mistress of the Prince Regent. After this happy match his fortunes were much improved. He became ostentatious and something of a beau. Robert Finch commented wryly in his diary that Nash was 'a great coxcombe,' adding: 'He is very fond of women . . . attempted even Mrs Parker, his wife's sister. He lives in Dover Street, has a charming place in the Isle of Wight and drives four horses.' Not that it matters. What Nash left us in Regent's Park, the Crescents and Terraces, the porticos and pediments, are of such gaiety and elegance as to make the heart sing. Despite hideous sodium lighting, these war-damaged Regency glories have been skilfully restored.

There is a tunnel running under the Marylebone Road, which links Park Crescent Gardens with Park Square Gardens opposite the Park proper. The purpose of this tunnel was to facilitate the pushing of prams by nannies without danger to their charges: an expensive indulgence for these rich babies because the Bakerloo line has to burrow deeper as a result. But the tunnel had another use. Comparatively private and unlit, it was the ideal rendezvous for soldiers from the Albany Street barracks who made assignations with the servant girls (perhaps even the nannies!) from the big houses in the district. Until the recent road-widening, there was a brood of spotted fly-catchers nesting in a shrubbery in these gardens. I wonder what became of them.

Those were the origins of the New Road, a broad boulevard in the continental manner. From Paddington to Tottenham Court it was in the charge of the Turnpike Trust, who cut down the trees, filled in the ditches, and erected post-and-rail fences. Seven watchmen were hired and equipped with horns and blunderbusses. Lamps were established at regular intervals with a lamplighter to keep them lit. But the Trust cut corners (as it were), and underpaid their employees, so that the watchmen, road labourers by day, fell asleep at night, and the lamps were not always ablaze.

There was just one church in the neighbourhood in these days – the Old Parish Church, as it was lovingly called. It had been built in 1741 on the site of the old medieval church, and was featured in *The Rake's Progress* (to be seen – and I do recommend a visit – at Sir John Soane's Museum in Lincoln's Inn Fields). It was architecturally almost nothing. 'A tiny brown-brick box with round-headed windows, flat broad gables and a little bell-turret at the west end.' (Summerson). It was approached along Lustie Lane, narrow and sinuous and part of the charming thoroughfare we now call Marylebone Lane. There was a tower just 31½ feet high and a wooden sundial, while in the yard stood a combined stocks and whipping post. On a slab as one entered could be seen the name of Humphrey Wanley, the antiquary, 'as honest a man and as learned a librarian as ever sat down to morning chocolate in velvet slippers'. In 1788 Charles Wesley was buried in the Churchyard at his own request and in 1803 Lady Hamilton's daughter by Nelson was baptised there, a hole-in-the-corner ceremony which was solomnised two years afterwards. But the Parish Church of St Mary's was inadequate to the needs of a fast-growing community. A letter in the *Gentleman's Magazine* for July 1807 confirms just how serious things were becoming: 'There is no font for baptism, no room for depositing the dead bodies on tressels, after the usual way, no aisle to contain them. They are placed in the most indecent manner in the pews. At the time I visited this scandal to our Church and nation, there were no fewer than five corpses placed in the manner described; eight children with their sponsors, etc., to be christened; and five women to be churched; all within these contracted dimensions. . . .'

The present St Mary's by Thomas Hardwick, an elegant Corinthian building with a portico and gilded caryatids, became the new Parish Church, having been erected in 1817 at a cost of £22,000, while the humble old building was pensioned off as the Parish Chapel, to be dismantled in 1949. The site is clearly marked on a plaque as 'The Old Church Garden', and very pleasant it is to sit in and dream of twelvepenny tarts and almond cheesecakes.

The style and status of the new church says much about upwardly mobile St Marylebone during the Regency period. It had a seating capacity of between three and four thousand. The president of the Royal Academy, Benjamin West, contributed an Annunciation and a Holy Family painted by himself. A generous gesture; one picture, he let it be known, would be a free gift. For the Annunciation, however, he charged the horified vestrymen the exorbitant sum of £800.

The Duke of Portland had not just a family pew but a whole wing, complete with a fireplace. Charles Wesley, the son of the hymn-writer who was retained to play privately for the Prince Regent, now played publicly to the fashionable congregation. There were three beadles and ten pew-openers to ensure that only those who knew how to behave and had been to respectable schools should be permitted to worship the Lord. Indeed, by the middle of the nineteenth century St Marylebone had become the richest parish in England.

Two hundred yards east, on the opposite side to Hardwick's Church, stands a 'Waterloo Church', built with money provided by an Act of Parliament as a thank-offering for the deliverance of the country from invasion by Napoleon. Holy Trinity, on the corner of Albany Street, is not without charm, but Sir John Soane's building, consecrated in 1828, seems to have lost its dignity. It is overlooked by the White House, a huge hotel and block of flats (where I once interviewed Miss UK in a negligée), and has become the headquarters and book-shop for the Society for Promoting Christian Knowledge, where it sells volumes of doctrine and dogma and cassettes to bring ease to troubled spirits. Bravely the building still celebrates Holy Communion at lunchtime every Tuesday. But it has two claims to fame. Church-fanciers will know it for its open-air pulpit built cunningly into the façade. And bibliophiles will recollect that here in the 1930s Allen Lane pioneered his Penguin Books from the crypt, which was also used as an air-raid shelter during World War Two.

Besides churches, Marylebone Road is notable for stations and travellers, clinics and invalids, courts and criminals, the headquarters of vast retailing operations, waxworks and stars, and music.

Baker Street Station is and was a hugely important one. When it

St Mary's Church.

opened in 1863 it was part of the Metropolitan Railway (Paddington Bishop's Road to Farringdon Street), the first urban underground line to be built anywhere in the world. *The Times,* in the rearguard of public opinion as usual, reckoned that it was 'an insult to common sense to suppose that people . . . would ever prefer . . . to be driven amid palpable darkness through the foul subsoil of London'. *The Times* was absolutely wrong.

Baker Street underground and the Metropolitan Railway has its own Laureate, of course – John Betjeman, a marvellous man, may he rest in peace:

Early Electric! Maybe even here
    They met that evening at six-fifteen
Beneath the hearts of this electrolier
    And caught the first non-stop to Willesden Green
Then out and on, through rural Rayner's Lane
To autumn-scented Middlesex again.

Cancer has killed him. Heart is killing her.
  The trees are down. An Odeon flashes fire
Where stood their villa by the murmuring fir
    When 'they would for their children's good conspire'.
Of all their loves and hopes on hurrying feet
Thou art the worn memorial, Baker Street.

The trains were powered solely by steam until 1905 when the first electric traction was introduced; there were three classes, two kinds of rolling stock, a mixed gauge and special trains for 'workmen' who paid three-pence as a return fare. Recently (April 1984) London Transport com-pleted the restoration of Baker Street to its original condition, or something close to it because the platforms may no longer be built of timber. It used to be possible – I'm talking now of my youth – to travel from Maidenhead to Baker Street, changing at Ealing Broadway, for the cost of a shilling ticket to the cartoon cinema. I could tell you how this was done, but it might be wiser to plead the fifth amendment!

Within the carapace of Baker Street Station is a curious cluster of little shops, but what they are doing there is a mystery. A more random collection could hardly be imagined. We have a boutique, improbably called Che Guevara (you start as a communist liberator, you end by selling T-shirts!), a Health and Beauty Studio, a hairdresser, a recruit-ment centre for London Transport, Mad Man Two Swords which sells souvenirs, Unilex Scottish Woollens, a small independent cinema, World Pearl Jewellers, and an old-fashioned gift centre selling, among other items, a punk dressed in a Union Jack.

A quarter of a mile to the west of the tube station is the real thing, Marylebone Station, built thirty-six years afterwards, and the last of the Metropolitan termini to be put up. Sir Edward William Watkin, an early proponent of the Channel tunnel, envisaged it as an essential link between the Midlands and the South Coast or even the Continent. But he faced powerful opposition from the residents of St John's Wood, who were always an influential and vocal bunch, not backward in coming forward. To give you some idea, nineteenth-century locals included the Duke of Wellington, Gladstone, Joseph Buonaparte the ex-King of Spain, Lord Lister of antiseptic fame, Florence Nightingale and Octavia Hill, who reformed nursing and housing respectively, and from the arts: Flaxman, Turner, Allan Ramsay, Leigh Hunt, Cruikshank and Charles Dickens, who seems to have lived everywhere. Anyway, the nobs and the MCC fiercely opposed Watkin's Great Central Railway, and the struggle cost him so much that he had no money left for an architect and had to employ a jobbing engineer from the site. The result was unspec-tacular but not unpleasing, although to build the station four and a half thousand inhabitants had to be rehoused, which is why there are so many

Baker Street Station.

enormous apartment blocks in the environs of Marylebone Station. Still standing to remind us of the quiet dignity of the station's design is the old Victoria buffet (now a bar) in which the original panelling and mirrors remain. It is altogether a *quiet* station, described by A. G. Macdonell in *England, Their England* as a place where 'porters go on tiptoe, where the barrows are rubber-tyred and the trains sidle mysteriously in and out with only the faintest of toots on their whistles, so as not to disturb the signalmen'. But if British Rail has its callous way nothing will remain of Marylebone Station.

In front of it stands the Hotel Grand Central (1897–9), which was imposingly appointed with seven hundred rooms, each having a fire-place. When it opened it would have cost you fifteen shillings per day to stay there. One of its unique features was a cycle track on the roof, but as the years passed there were few who could remember just what it was for. Wounded officers were lodged there during the First World War, and during the Second, it was a de-briefing station for those courageous men who had escaped concentration camps. Now it is the headquarters of the British Railways Board, but it, like the Station, is very much at risk. When will they ever learn?

Marylebone Road forms the northern boundary of where people are

poorly. Along the south side there are hospitals, clinics and discarded medical dressings in the gutters. But Regent's Park represents a healthy body in a healthy mind. In Marylebone Road is the Samaritan Hospital for Women, founded in 1847 as the Gynaepathic Institute Free Hospital. Adjoining it is the Western Ophthalmic Hospital, founded in 1856 as the St Marylebone Eye and Ear Institution (the site used to house a shooting box for King George III and his guests). Both hospitals, enabling you to make babies and to see them properly, are a part of the St Mary's Hospital Paddington Group. Travelling east you reach the London Clinic, an unusual private hospital founded in 1932. It is unusual in that it has no doctors, merely providing ancillary services, consulting rooms and operating theatres. It is also unusual in that despite the wealth of many of its patients – e.g. the Duke of Windsor, Charlie Chaplin, Elizabeth Taylor and King Hussein – it is non-profit making. Beyond it to the east lies Harley Street, where the wealthiest doctors flirt and flatter and cajole, and where Equity, the Actors Union, lies like a beached whale, beyond the help of medical science. And further towards the rising sun, in Euston Road, is the Wellcome Foundation for scientific and medical research, and the Elizabeth Garrett Anderson Hospital, managed entirely by and for women and threatened in the seventies with closure. Elizabeth Anderson (née Garrett) was an extraordinary person. In 1856 at the age of twenty she announced that she was going to become a doctor. But at the Middlesex Hospital, where she was a probationary nurse, the other students refused to permit her to enter the dissecting room, and the Senate of London University refused her application to be examined for matriculation. But she took her MD in Paris, was elected a member of the BMA in 1872, bore three children, and became Mayor of Aldeburgh. The surgeon at the hospital in the early years of this century was Louisa Aldrich-Blake, the first woman to gain the degree of Master of Surgery.

Confirming the links between medicine and the Church in Marylebone Road, the rector of St Mary's, Christopher Hamel-Cooke, has plans to turn the crypt into a place where invalids are helped to come to terms with the nature of their sickness. The plans will involve the NHS working alongside a priest, and are now well-advanced, although it took a year to clear the crypt of coffins and skeletons. Already the laying on of hands is practised in the church on the first Sunday of each month. The church is also to have an organ transplant, for the Royal Academy of Music across the road is raising funds to acquire a splendid new instrument, so that the church will resound with organ music while the lame throw away their crutches.

Left: The Hotel Grand Central, built in 1897–9, but now used as the headquarters of the British Railways Board.

The Academy itself, founded in 1822, is now sited in a dignified building considerably influenced by Wren, and contains a new library of full orchestral scores of modern works for the use of its six hundred and twenty-five students. An early professor was the eminent Henry Bishop, who wrote 'Home Sweet Home' and was the first British composer to be knighted. Sir Henry Bishop? I cannot believe that you have never heard of him!

The Academy and the neighbouring impressively gabled flats known as Harley House were both built in 1910 on the site of the Old Harley House, a private residence of great éclat built behind a walled garden. It was in 1856 that this house was rented by the expatriate Queen of Oudh with the Oudh Royal Family and a hundred and ten royal retainers, who camped in the garden. Not surprisingly the locals objected.

The Marylebone Magistrates' Court is 'in an insignificant Italianate style, but characteristic as illustrating the modest scale of public buildings in the borough three generations ago'. (Pevsner). But it has a reputation to bely its modest architecture. A. C. Plowden was the stipendiary there in the twenties, a man celebrated for his wisdom, wit and humanity, 'whose sayings so frequently delighted the readers of the Periodical Press'. During the 1960s and 70s Mr Romain presided over the Number One Court and was known as the kindest magistrate in London. It was his practice to fine cannabis offenders a sum of money roughly equivalent to the cost of the dope. His place has now been taken by the handsome Mr Fanner. On the evidence of the morning I spent in court, things continue to be in safe hands.

I listened to the hearing of a case in which a young panel-beater was picked up by a well-known local prostitute, who agreed a fee of £20. The panel-beater took her to the garage in which he was working and had his way with her. It then turned out – for he turned out his pockets – that he was a fiver short. The girl was extremely cross, but it wasn't until she started attacking the newly beaten panel upon which he had been working that he lost his temper and struck her in the face, splitting her lip and causing her nose to bleed. 'Cars, you see, are his first love,' explained the defending council. The man was fined £50 with £50 compensation for the bloody nose. It was decided to pay the compensation to the court, for the victim 'is here more often than anywhere else!'

The courts were erected on a site that had adjoined the Royal Apollo Saloon, which in its turn was next to the celebrated Yorkshire Stingo. The Saloon, which was opened in 1836, attracted huge crowds to its plays and concerts. Here too were bowling greens, May Day sports, and in 1836 and 1837 balloon ascents. Another old pub was the Globe Tavern which still survives on the corner of Baker Street. In an upstairs room huge portions of saltless food are served by genial but chaotic Australians.

As you can see, the religious, the mobile, the sick and those who attend them, the musical and the criminal, are all catered for in this road. But the general impression given to the pedestrian who walks along the broad but polluted thoroughfare is of people making money. Thus along the north side we find Woolworth House, National Cash Registers, Marathon House (originally Burmah-Castrol House), Lloyds Bank (incorporated into Berkeley Court, which has a fine roof garden covering an acre) and Albany Terrace soon to be offices; along the south side, the head offices for British Home Stores, Heron House, Ferguson House, notable for a stone frieze of Dickensian characters, for this is the site of 1 Devonshire Terrace where Dickens and his large family lived; also the Nat West and the Inspectorate of Taxes. It is intriguing to see Woolworths and the BHS in opposition. Frank Winfield Woolworth opened his first London store in 1924, his policy being to sell all goods at just three prices: sixpence, threepence, and one penny. Four years later British Home Stores were launched with a top price of a shilling, although soon afterwards the ceiling was raised to five shillings to permit the selling of upholstery, curtains and carpets. Today Woolworth's is capitalised at £657.4 million and British Home Stores at £637.9 million.

Despite these huge conglomerate offices, and the even huger apartment buildings – Burmah House, with its dead trees and its vast white fire escape; Chiltern Court, where H. G. Wells, Hughie Greene, and my Auntie lived or live; Nottingham Terrace, Ulster Place, Portman and Bickenhall Mansions – Marylebone Road remains a home for eccentrics. It was from the Edgware Road end that George Shillibeer ran his omnibus service. To sit inside a 'Shillibus' cost eighteen pence, to sit on top sixpence less, and that charge included the use of a newspaper. The omnibus was drawn by three horses trotting abreast and the conductors were men of good breeding, some even the sons of naval officers. Still in the road is E. Gandolfi (No. 150) – well, he has only been there for thirty-seven years – where you can buy ballet shoes and tutus, leotards and leg-warmers. The shop-fittings are original. One can also find The World Development Company (No. 152) and at No. 146 Hidden Hearing, where you can buy 'the world's smallest hearing aids'. The huge picture of President Reagan in the window suggests that perhaps he too wears one. Also, of course, in Marylebone is another American President, or the head of one. The handsome copper face of John F. Kennedy (1917–63) stares out rather wearily at the endless traffic from between a magnolia and a Japanese quince. Behind him a car park and builders' skips; plenty of symoblism there to work on. The sculpture by Jacques Lipchitz was paid for by more than fifty thousand *Daily Telegraph* readers and unveiled by Bobby. Not far from Hidden Hearing is the Body Clinic ('men only, massage, sauna') and then the German Bedding Centre. Next to that the Alba London Luggage Centre and the seedy-looking Arizona Club. A curious grouping.

But the greatest eccentric of the Marylebone Road is the woman who, despite having been dead for 135 years, still brings two million tourists a year

The queue for Madame Tussaud's.

to this thriving by-pass, fourteen thousand of them recently in a single day. I
mean, of course, Anne Marie Grosheltz, better known as Madame Tussaud.
Consider her extraordinary life. Born in Strasbourg, she never knew her
father, who may have been a soldier or, possibly, the German doctor and
wax-modeller Dr Curtius. Her mother becomes the doctor's housekeeper,
and Curtius teaches Marie, as she is known, the mystical techniques of
modelling in wax. Her talent is such that she is appointed art-tutor to the
sister of King Louis XV, and sets up residence in the Palace of Versailles.
Curtius, skilled in sensing which way the wind is blowing, is amongst the
enfants de la patrie who storm the Bastille. Marie too survives the terror, but

it is her gruesome task to model the decapitated heads of her recent
employers and friends. Just how gruesome the work became is powerfully
described in Marie's memoirs. This concerns Robespierre:

> When he found that he had no means of escaping execution, he endeavoured
> with a pistol to blow out his brains, but only shattered his under jaw, which
> was obliged to be tied up when he was taken to the scaffold. The executioner
> when about to do his office, tore the dressing roughly away, and Robespierre
> uttered a piercing shriek, as his lower jaw separated from the upper, whilst his
> blood flowed copiously. His head presented a most dreadful spectacle, and
> immediately after death it was taken to the Madeleine, where Madame
> Tussaud took a cast of it, from which the likeness she now possesses was
> taken.

In 1802, Curtius having died, Marie, who has married a civil engineer
and given birth to three children, brings Dr Curtius' exhibition, now hers, to
London and exhibits it at the Lyceum Theatre. But the show is advertised as
a Phantasmagoria, featuring her husband's optical illusions, with the wax
figures a subsidiary attraction. Success comes when Marie begs permission to
be allowed to take a death mask of Colonel Despard (beheaded for attempting to assassinate George III), and, having done so, exhibits it. Her strong
stomach and the macabre tastes of the public make independence possible,
and she leaves her husband and sets off for twenty-six years of touring in
Britain. In 1835 she settles the exhibition permanently at The Bazaar in
Baker Street, dying fifteen years later at the age of ninety. Until her death,
the staunch and resolute old girl had sat at the box office of her exhibition
counting the money. But now her descendants take on the running of the
exhibition, which moves to the Marylebone Road in 1884. As recently as
1967 Bernard Tussaud, the last of the dynasty and great-great-grandson of
Marie, died.

I visited the wax-works a few days ago. Modern techniques have been
applied to the old skills. 'The Battle of Trafalgar', with gunfire and smoke, as
seen from the lower decks of the *Victory*, assails the senses, not least the
nostrils, with the pungent odour of Stockholm Tar and rope. The Beatles (by
no means the most successful models) cluster round a player piano pro-
grammed with their hits. Other superstars, such as Bowie and Boy George,
sing and speak with characteristic insouciance. Backstage in the modelling
studio, I was confronted with trays of glass eyes, severed heads, and the
naked figure of Martina Navratilova. Next door in the Planetarium the huge
projector by Carl Zeiss of Oberkochen gives an accurate representation of
some nine thousand stars, all of them authentically graded as to brightness.
Also in the Planetarium, laser rock shows, improvised to seventies music
(notably Pink Floyd), explore the increasingly intriguing possibilities of laser
pyrotechnics. But I have to confess that both my children and myself took as
much pleasure from the end-of-pier slot machines and the distorting mirrors

as from the Battle of Trafalgar and the interplanetary wonders of the universe.

From cattle-drovers to Pink Floyd, from bowling greens to Woolworths, from Tyburn gallows to the laying-on of hands, the New Road has survived. From fly-over to underpass, acrid with pollution in mid-summer, treacherous with black ice in mid-winter, it cuts a swathe between the fashionable haunts of Hampstead and St John's Wood and the bustling office-workers of the West End. The ghosts of Robespierre and Marat mingle with Jack the Ripper and Garry Gilmore, rich invalids with young musicians, millionaires with petty criminals. There are worse places to be stuck in traffic jams.

Left: Ken Livingstone, GLC Leader, as modelled for Madame Tussaud.

A general view of Old Compton Street.

2

Old Compton Street

They don't get no spaghetti

Old Compton Street
Frankie Blake

In the West End of London about half a mile long
Is the rendezvous of a very cosmopolitan throng
With its shops and flats so clean and so neat,
You've guessed it! Right first time! It's Old Compton Street.

It's got five pubs and sex shops galore
Thank Christ it's no longer or we'd have a few more.
Of delicatessens there's not many – just about two –
For in a street half a mile long that'll just about do.

The restaurants vary and there's quite a few:
French, Indian, Italian, Chinese and Smithy's the fish and chip too.
But let me give you a warning and a bit of advice:
Before you dine in any of them, just check the price.

Soho is bounded to the north by Oxford Street, to the east by the
Charing Cross Road, to the south by Coventry Street, and to the west by
Regent Street. No buses run through it. Despite its notorious reputation,
it is rare to see policemen in Soho and, when you do, they are usually
alone.

In the days of the Sabini gang and the silk-stocking murders, it was a
rough area. During the war there were plenty of 'spivs' and 'kerb-boys'
operating, as well as 'dippers' and 'whizzers' after your wallet. But apart
from these misdemeanours and the sly pawnbroking swindles carried out
by 'Moyshe the mobster', the only notable recorded disturbance of the
peace was the gruesome Tony Mella murder in Dean Street, a murder in
settlement of an unpaid debt followed by a suicide, as I recall.

Within Soho, which has been colonised by Flemish weavers,
Huguenots, French emigré priests fleeing from the Terror, Belgians,
Italians, Jews bruised from the Cossack pogroms, and the Chinese, each
notable street has taken on a different character. Little Pulteney Street,
where early this century every third house was a brothel, was nick-named

Knaves' Acre. Wardour Street, known as 'the Street' and less engagingly as 'the only street in the world that's shady on both sides', is the centre of what remains of the British cinema industry. Archer Street has long been the place where itinerant musicians congregate in the expectation (but musicians are a gloomy bunch) of a hastily organised gig or session. It's fallen on hard times, has Archer Street. Great Windmill Street was, of course, for lovers of the female form, but was also emphatically Jewish for Jack Solomons had his gym there, and to it came all the boxing champions, Dempsey and Tunney and the handsome Carpentier, while Jack Isow's kosher restaurant at the top of the street was for goyim as well as mensch with plenty of schleppers always in evidence. It was Jack Isow who, when faced with anti-semitism at a restaurant outside London, bought the restaurant. Frith Street (originally *Thrift* Street) was – and is – for eating and jazz, while Gerrard Street and the lively area between Shaftesbury Avenue and Coventry Street are London's Chinatown.

Soho has almost no surviving buildings of architectural interest – only the House of St Barnabas at No. 1 Greek Street deserves more than a cursory glance – which is something of a relief in a London crammed with listed buildings. In Soho it's the people you look at, and the people look at you. It seems central to Londoners, but you need only go back four hundred years and you find that it was not a part of London at all. According to Ralph Agas's map, Soho was fields of pasture with grazing cattle; a woman (somewhere near St Anne's Churchyard) is drying her linen in the sun. The only thoroughfares were Oxford Street, identified as 'The Waye to Uxbridge', St Martin's Lane, which was just a meandering lane; and a road approximating roughly to Shaftesbury Avenue marked 'The Way to Redinge', which is certainly not the route I would recommend to Reading, but there you are. In the area of Drury Lane was the village of St Giles; there was the walled-in Convent (sic) Garden; and there were splendid mansions in the Strand with gardens down to the Thames. Apart from these, and a few houses to the north of St James's Park, there was no development in the 'West End' except Westminister.

There have been many learned papers on the origin of the name Soho, which is odd because learned papers are really not needed. Sohoe Fields were good hunting territory, and So-Ho (with variations) was the acknowledged cry of the huntsman after his victim. There is even in Soho Square a small edifice believed to have been a hunting lodge used by Charles II. There is no point in looking further for the origin of the name. Yet there remain those who point out that 'So-Ho!' was the battle cry of the followers of the unfortunate Duke of Monmouth at Sedgemoor (1685); unfortunate because a few days later he was beheaded.

The Duke of Monmouth lived at Monmouth House, on the site of which the Hospital For Women stands, with its ominous sign: 'Please Go Quietly'. It was concerning Monmouth that Aphra Behn wrote:

Young Jemmy was a lad
  of Royal Birth and Breeding
With every Beauty Clad:
  And ev'ry Grace Exceeding;
A face and shape so wondrous fine,
  So Charming ev'ry part;
That every Lass upon the Green
  For Jemmy had a Heart.

Monmouth was a promoter of Soho, but the area was called Soho long before his death at Sedgemoor. Some believe 'Soho' to be a corruption of Soe Hoe, meaning South Hill, but Soho is certainly not a hill. Some fanatics argue that 'So Ho!' means 'Stop' or 'Hold Your Horses!' and refers to a movement to eliminate any more building development in the area, yet when the name was first used there was no building development in the area. Enough said.

From its beginnings in the last quarter of the seventeenth century, Soho was always a place in which immigrants settled, and Old Compton Street the main shopping and trading centre. By 1710 more than a quarter of the Old Compton Street ratepayers were French. By 1793, of seventy-eight houses in the street, only seven or eight were without shop-fronts, and some of those seven or eight were taverns. To give an idea of the range of services offered, along the north side there were: a baker, a broker, a cabinet-maker, a carpenter, a carver and gilder, a china merchant, a cloth merchant, a coal merchant, a confectioner, a gold-beater, a goldsmith and jeweller, a haberdasher, a hairdresser, an iron-monger, an oilman (!), a perfumer, a pianoforte-maker, three publicans, two tallow wax-chandlers, a tinman, an upholsterer and a whitesmith. By 1840 every house had a shop-front although none of those 1840 fronts now remains. By 1900 half the inhabitants of Old Compton Street were foreign, and continental, socialist and anarchist publications were freely available.

It was also a street which attracted the talented, the Bohemian, and the weird. At No. 37 lived Thomas Walker, the actor who created Macheath for John Gay. And later the same house was occupied by Giacobbe Cervetto, the violin-cellist, who advertised his compositions for sale at that address. (Cervetto lived to the age of a hundred and three and left £50,000 to his son in 1783.) In the 1680s Peter Berault, author of *A Nosegay or Miscellany of several Divine Truths* gave lessons in French and Latin from 'Cumpton street, in Soo-Hoo Fields, four doors of the Myter', while Mr Fert, Dancing Master, who advertised in the *Tatler* (1710) that he had composed 'a new Dance called The Toumay' and who was prepared to give terpsichorean instruction 'at Persons of Quality's Houses, and others, at a reasonable rate' was based in Old Compton

Street. Next to The Golden Key lived Isaac van den Helm, a Dutch Tablemaker, whose fine painted tea tables were guaranteed to endure boiling hot water. And Schiefer, stay-maker to Her Majesty in 1771, had a splendid stock including: 'Pompadours, jesuits, brunswicks, robes, suits, sacques, gowns, young ladies' robes and slips, riding habits, and masquerade dresses'. Nicholas Sprimont, the proprietor of the Chelsea China Manufactory, lived here between 1742 and 1770. So too in 1778 did John Leland, probably the author of the delightful *Fanny Hill.* George Wombwell the menagerist and Mr Jobson whose puppet shows incensed the authorities set up their businesses in Old Compton Street. Wombwell's story is an impressive one. In the early 1900s he had a boot and shoe-maker's shop. One day at the London Docks he saw some of the first boa-constrictors to be imported into England and, having always owned small animals and having a feeling for them, offered £75 for a pair of the snakes, other potential purchasers being understandably wary. Within three weeks he had already covered his investment with public displays, and at the time of his death, he owned upwards of twenty lions, five elephants, smaller animals without number, and also three establishments, more than forty caravans, and a dray-horse stud of between a hundred and ten and a hundred and twenty horses.

In 1778 at the Compton Street Exhibition Room a mock-trial took place in a 'true Representation of a Court of Judicature' – admission half a crown. The case being heard was that old chestnut, whether the Chevalier D'Eon was a man or a woman. (After his death at the age of eighty-two a medical tribunal attested that he was indeed a man, but he had dressed as a woman to indulge a whim of Marie Antoinette.) The first black swans to be imported into Britain (from Botany Bay by Sir Joseph Banks) stayed with Mr Latham in Old Compton Street and from the windpipes of these extraordinary creatures were formed 'the softest and most harmonious sounds ever yet heard'. Exotic too were Verlaine and Rimbaud who drank Pernod in a bar at No. 5 and gave readings of their dissolute poems. Mr Talma, dentist and father of the French tragedian, lived at No. 55 in 1773, while two years earlier poor Chatelaine, the engraver, had died in penury just a stone's throw away and been buried by his friends in the poor-ground of the Portland Street Workhouse. (And there was a Pest House and Leper-colony on the site of what today is Carnaby Street, but tourists are not alerted to that!) Richard Wagner was a resident, and Frederick Accum, who is less well known than Richard Wagner but altogether more useful, being a German chemist who was influential in bringing gas-lighting to London. But I am running ahead of myself. It had been my intention to write

Left: Much of the modern image of Old Compton Street is a long way from the diversity of its eighteenth-century inhabitants.

about the Compton family after whom the street was named, and, the story being such a remarkable one, so I shall.

Old Compton Street was named after the Earl of Northampton, who owned much of the land, but New Compton Street was named after Henry Compton, his son, the Bishop of London. Spencer Compton, the Earl, was killed at the Battle of Hopton Heath, in 1643. Henry was the sixth and youngest son and destined, as was the fashion with youngest sons, for the Church. The Comptons remained staunchly royalist during the Commonwealth and greeted Charles II on his return to the capital. Henry had been travelling in Italy and with the Stuarts back in power he returned to England and resumed his studies. He took his MA at Oxford in 1662, and his MA at Cambridge in 1666. Within three more years he was a doctor of divinity and within four the Bishop of London, a position he was to hold for thirty-eight years. He was much loved and, wrote Evelyn, 'like to make a grave and serious good man', but he had one short-coming – he was no use in the pulpit. Together with Sancroft, his Dean at St Paul's, he stood by Wren when the great architect was having desperate problems rebuilding the Cathedral. Compton himself was responsible for St Anne's, Soho, in those days – nothing of the original survives – regarded as a precious architectural gem. Before performing the dedication of the new church, Compton characteristically took pains to ensure that all the workmen, the builders, the masons and the carpenters, had been fully paid for their time and trouble. The Bishop was popular, successful and in favour with the King, who appointed him tutor to his two nieces, an onerous responsibility since one was to become Queen Mary and the other Queen Anne.

With the accession of James II, Henry Compton's star began to wane. A certain Dr Sharp, Dean of Norwich and Rector of St Giles's-in-the-Field, preached a powerful sermon against the Roman faith – behaviour which the King had specifically forbidden. Compton, who was no great lover of Rome, was commanded to suspend Sharp, but explained that while he could (and would) request him not to preach again for a while in London, he had no jurisdiction over how Sharp preached in his own Cathedral of Norwich. The formidable Judge Jeffreys punished Compton by relieving him of all his spiritual duties, but he could not prevent him from worshipping in his own Church of St Anne's, which he did, together with many fashionable and influential Londoners, including an ex-mistress of King James who took a regular pew. At about that time Sancroft, who had been appointed Archbishop of Canterbury, and six other bishops refused publicly to proclaim the King's 'Declaration of Liberty of Conscience', and were tried and acquitted. Now Compton and the six bishops sent an invitation to William of Orange and his wife Mary to come to England. The Princess Anne, whom Compton had instructed in the Anglican doctrine, determined to flee the country, but

the Thames bridges were all under guard. Compton replaced his episcopal vestments with the uniform of a Life Guards officer and rode to
Nottingham in the front of a carriage, in which Anne was secretly
installed. There a local militia was set up with the responsibility of
protecting the person of the Princess, and the Bishop was appointed to be
Captain of the Guard.

In due course Compton was to be rewarded for his courage and
diligence by conducting the Coronation of William and Mary in Westminster Abbey, but he never became Primate, for, when the Arch-
bishopric fell vacant, Tillotson, Dean of St Paul's, a whig, a noted
scholar, and an inspired preacher, got the job. Living now in Fulham
Palace, as was traditional for Bishops of London, Compton never aban-
doned his Soho connections, and shortly before he died preached in St
Anne's to a congregation which almost certainly included the children
and grandchildren of the man who had built the church for him. His text:
'Let your moderation be known to all men.'

But the church has not survived. The tower became dangerous and
was replaced in 1806. The remainder of the church was bombed in 1940.
As I write these words, preparatory work is being undertaken by the Soho
Society to develop the site. Two thousand skeletons have to be removed
from what is now the car-park and taken to Surrey. Then nineteen flats,
two shops, a museum, and a crèche will be built, with the car park
underneath. The raised gardens, an oasis for derelicts and over-burdened
city workers alike, will, of course, remain. Dorothy L. Sayers was, for
many years, a churchwarden of St Anne's. Her ashes are interred there
and a portrait of her hangs in the tower.

The Duke of Monmouth and Henry Compton were two who helped to
give Soho a distinction and a chic in the early days of its history. A third
was Mrs Cornelys, and her story is so curious that it deserves a page or
two, despite that she lived in Soho Square and not Old Compton Street.

Born in Venice in 1723, she was the daughter of an actor named Imer.
Aged seventeen, Teresa Imer became the mistress of Senator Malipiero,
and after an unimportant marriage to a dancer – maybe she was in love –
formed a further liaison with the Margrave of Baireuth. A margrave was a
governor, one up on a senator. Bored with Vienna, in which she lived as
Madame Pompeati, and with Amsterdam, where she married a Mr
Cornelis de Rigerboos, she became a theatre manager and singer,
although a contemporary records that 'she had such a masculine and
violent manner of singing that few female symptoms were perceptible'.
In London she found scope for most of her talents and not only organised
a series of musical soirées at Carlisle House (from 1760) but bore her
lover, Casanova, a daughter. Her soirées became increasingly colourful
and fashionable; profitable, too, with six hundred guests paying two
guineas a head. She hung blue and yellow satin on the walls. She

installed primitive air conditioning ('tea below stairs and ventilators above', said the advertisements) and galas, concerts, masquerades and festivals succeeded one another with dazzling frequency throughout the season. One 'lady of high quality' appeared at a masquerade, dressed as an Indian Princess wearing jewels to the value of £100,000. With her was a suite of three young black female slaves holding her train, and two young black male slaves supporting a canopy over her head. The Duchess of Kingston appeared in the guise of Iphygenia, 'looking,' remarked Horace Walpole, 'in a state of almost ready for the sacrifice'. Mrs Cornelys would illuminate Carlisle House with four thousand wax candles and hire a hundred musicians to play. Cutpurses were everywhere. By now Teresa could boast three secretaries, a confidante, a dumb attendant, thirty-two servants, and six horses. Occasionally she gave the proceeds of a ball to the poor people of the parish.

But success breeds jealousy, and Almack's, the smart club in St James's with its ninety-foot ballroom, challenged Mrs Cornelys's right to run her establishment. Information was laid against her as a disorderly person and she was fined £50, while the Italian Opera House pulled strings to have her chief singer, Guadani, arrested. Other Soho Square residents complained about the noise of carriages at night, and the parties came to an end. In December 1772 the House and everything in it was put up to auction (no entry without a catalogue) and Mrs Cornelys retired from public life. At least she did for more than twenty years. But then in 1795 she installed herself in Knightsbridge and advertised herself as a 'Vendor of Asses' milk', but 'her taste had not adapted itself to the vagaries of fashion', and she was forced to seek asylum from her creditors within the Rules of the Fleet Prison. On 19 August 1797, she died there aged seventy-four. The ballroom of Carlisle House became a Roman Catholic chapel; the house itself was demolished in 1788 and on the site stands St Patrick's church.

It really is remarkable when one considers just how influential Soho has been during its short history in matters political and artistic. Mozart gave concerts in Frith Street, and Macaulay lodged there when he first came to London. Others with Soho connections include Augustus John, Dylan Thomas, Sickert, Dali, Tambimuttu, Canaletto, Louis Macneice, John Logie Baird (who invented television at Bianchi's in Frith Street), De Quincy with his orphaned nine-year-old girl friend, Sheraton, Thomas Lawrence and Gainsborough, Charles Lamb and William Blake (born at 28 Broad Street), Casanova and Sarah Siddons, Mrs Meyrick, Dryden, Reynolds, Burke, Bolingbroke, Becky Sharp, Dr Manette, Angelica Kauffmann, Hazlitt and Horace Walpole, Theodore the ex-king of Corsica who pledged his kingdom against his debts and lost, and Oscar Wilde.

At Kettners, Edward VII would share one of the private rooms with

Opening oysters at Wheeler's.

Lily Langtry, and once, at Leoni's Quo Vadis Restaurant, Jascha Heifetz, the great violinist, inquired if Leoni could find a piano player to accompany him at a charity concert. Einstein was recommended, and readily agreed, but, during the performance, came in late after the cadenza. 'What's the matter with you?' muttered Heifetz (or so the story goes), 'can't you count?' 'Well,' Einstein replied, 'all things are relative, aren't they?'

Leoni's at 26 Dean Street – the first Soho restaurant I can remember visiting – is a fascinating place. The building was the home of Karl Marx when he arrived in London. The Quo Vadis was opened in 1926, by Leoni, who nineteen years previously had come as a boy to seek his fortune. He died in 1969, but the staff include many members of his family. 'If they don't work,' he was quoted as saying, 'then they don't get no spaghetti.' In an upstairs room Leoni once found a library of Karl Marx's research materials.

A parallel case is that of Bernard Walsh, the founder of Wheeler's in

Old Compton Street. He was born in Whitstable, where the oysters come from and where his father sold cockles and whelks. The Old Compton Street premises were bought as a sorting house for the oysters he sold to the big hotels. As word went round, young men and women rather the worse for wear would look in for oysters to cure their hangovers, and Bernard opened a bar to accommodate them. Then came the war and the stringent rationing regulations which insisted that, if you wished to eat rationed foods, you were not permitted to spend more than five shillings. But oysters were not rationed, so Wheeler's flourished where other restaurants foundered. After the war the upstairs extension was opened ('It had been a brothel,' I was told by the maitre d'hotel on a recent visit, 'but I did not tell you this until your lady visited the toilets') and other branches in London and Brighton followed. The menu at all Wheeler's restaurants is the same, and the dover sole meunière with spinach is the wisest choice. The Compton Street Wheeler's is enhanced with paintings bought from local art galleries. They reflect Bernard Walsh's three preoccupations: the sea, horse-racing and greyhound coursing.

Yet another celebrated feature of Old Compton Street is The French House just a few yards off Old Compton Street, but near as dammit, at 49 Dean Street. Originally the York Minister, it was always called The French House, until the demotic became formalised. Monsieur Victor Berlemont founded it in 1914 and, when he died in 1951, his son Gaston inherited. Victor had a celebrated moustache that was a foot in length; Gaston's is comparable. Headquarters for the Free French in London during the last war, its walls are decorated with French cyclists, French vaudeville stars, French boxers, and entertainers including, among many others, Grock, Criqui, Siki and the Fratellinis. But it was Victor's boast that no celebrity was to have his or her picture on the wall until he or she had had a drink in the York Minister. No pint mugs are available; shorts, champagne and wine are encouoraged. Visit it at lunch-time for what remains of London's Bohemian society. The admen can be identified by their strenuous efforts to look Bohemian. Philatelists get perforated there.

Other Old Compton Street pubs include the Three Greyhounds, the Coach and Horses (Whitbread) at No. 2, where some such inn or post-house has existed since at least 1731, and the Swiss Hotel (Charrington) at No. 53, which has lost its fine mansard roof and its twisted faience columns and its dormer gables, but still has a vaguely Renaissance Pan playing defiant pipes in buff-coloured terra-cotta. It has a reputation for toughness – 'the only pub in London where the rats eat the mice' – with an ex-Detective Inspector amongst its landlords. Also note the Admiral Duncan (Younger) at No. 54, popular with music publishers, and, after a chequered history, the winner of the Pub of the Year award given by the Soho Society's newspaper, *Soho Clarion*.

So far as eating and drinking is concerned, one need never budge beyond Old Compton Street. Although far grander breakfasts may be enjoyed at the Connaught (wear a tie, order the kedgeree), or Claridges, or the Waldorf (stewed figs and a massive buffet amidst high camp 1920s decor), Patisserie Valerie (No. 44) is just the place for freshly baked croissants and delicious coffee. Around you, you may spot romantically inclined office workers who stare into one another's eyes as their butter melts, and as you breakfast, sensational cream cakes are carried to the window displays, ready for lunch-time temps, starved of love. Valerie's cream cakes are now seriously challenged by the pastry cook at the Amalfi (No. 31) opposite, whose Gaggia Cappucino coffee, sprinkled with chocolate grains, is not to be lightly dismissed. And a few baguettes away at 28 Greek Street, Maison Bertaux is as mouth-wateringly creamy and flaky as ever.

For lunch the Soho Brasserie is that familiar phenomenon, an attempt to provide chic and fashionable eating at chic and fashionable prices, through the use of trendily casual waiters and waitresses and food cooked with unlikely combinations of ingredients. The reservation entries in the diary are more impressive than the customers actually on display there. Nonetheless it encourages coffee and cocktail drinkers as well as serious drinks, and money has been spent on dressing it appropriately. I give it three years.

There's not a great deal to be said on behalf of the Presto Pizza, Sniffy's Fish and Chips, Wimpy, the Cafe Espana, Alpha One (fish and chips and kebabs, and it is open very very late), Fatso's, the Hashmir Tandoori, or the Polo Bar; but Malaysian and Singapore restaurants – the Singapore Mandarin, the Desaru, and the Equatorial – suggest that Chinatown is moving up-market as it spreads north. Shaftesbury Avenue is becoming oriental and Old Compton Street already offers a firm of Chinese accountants (Tsen and Company at No. 35). I wish I could tell you something about Cheong's 'Clansman Charity European Association', which sounds intriguing, but I can't.

Breakfast, then, at Valerie's; a drink at the French House; lunch at the Brasserie or at Mama's, an American-style Jewish delicatessen with splendid salt-beef on rye, or at the 1970s style Bistingo; tea at Bertaux or the Amalfi; and dinner at Leoni's. But that sounds expensive, and Old Compton Street is not only a famous shopping street, but especially celebrated for its food shops, so that those who eat locally at home can do so in grand style.

Many have gone. A Gomez Ortega where you could buy Spanish sausages is gone. Parmigiani Figlio, Gennani, King Bomba, Chierico are four Italian stores which survived the blitz, but are now just happy memories and entries in archives. Parmigiani was the latest to go. Gone too is the Compton Fruit Stores, managed by Joe Lucas, who covered his

I. Camisa, *one of the celebrated food shops.*

baldness with a Basque beret, had run a dance band at Maxim's in Juan-Les-Pins, and once delivered a customer's baby amongst the cauliflowers and peaches. Di Lorenzo at No. 34 is now Mario's, whose windows groan with stuffed olives and aubergines, with tortillas and lasagne, with smoked salmon and with sea food. I. Camisa supplies home-made pasta, dry lentils and olive oil, and Garmis specialises in preserved meats and salamis, fresh egg pasta, cheeses, mushrooms and squid. Vinorio ('In Vinorio Veritas') serves Grissini, Ricard chocolate, pasta and olive oil as well as Italian wines. For wine, Del Monico's (No. 64) was the first discount wine store in London, and remains as competitive as ever, but it has to be for Gerry's, the Old Compton Street Wine Bar, and the

P. Denny, catering outfitters for a hundred and twenty years.

Vintage House are chivvying at its heels. Coffee has always been available in specialist stores in Old Compton Street, the original being the
Algerian Coffee Stores, supplying wine and coffee grinders and percola-
tors, as well as ten kinds of coffees, and teas with exotic names like
Gunpowder Green and Peach-flavoured Oolong, although nothing, so
far as I know, is from Algeria. The Algerian Coffee Stores runs an
international mail order service. Now there is also Cawardines, almost
next door, and A. Angelucci, just round the corner in Frith Street.
Bifulco, the continental butchers, is deservedly celebrated. It supplies
many of the best known West End restaurants and hotels with continental cuts and ready-to-cook kebabs, but for the private shopper it offers

chicken escalopes at a modest thirty pence, chicken kiev at just ninety pence a spurt, and glamorous sausages. Those who regret the passing of Benoit Bulcke can take comfort here.

Other celebrated Old Compton Street shops which have survived include Moroni & Sons, P. Denny & Co., Coleman Cohens, the Cigar Shop, and the English and Continental Pharmacy. Moroni's (No. 48) is now run by the third generation of the Moroni dynasty, and its *raison d'etre* now and always is to stock and sell foreign language newspapers. The names of continental newspapers and magazines have always struck insular me as wonderfully romantic. *La Stampa, Il Tempo, Corbiere della Sera, Der Spiegel, Inconnu, Marie Claire, Freundin, Quick, Oggi, Brave, Benissimo, Sport Intrepido, Uomo Mare, Elle* . . . Is it possible that to an Italian the *Daily Telegraph* or *The Economist* or *Newsweek* has the same ring? Surely not.

Moroni & Son was also one of the first newsagents to run an information board. In 1946 you could, by acting upon it, have acquired a pair of double-bed sheets; a Siamese cat; a dinner jacket and three dress-shirts; an accordion going cheap (there's a joke there somewhere!); and 'first-class button-holes made by hand'. You could also have found work as a floor man (£1 a day), a waitress, a cleaner or a washer-up. Until recently there was competition at No. 53 from S. Solosy, who has a splendid book shop in the Charing Cross Road. But foreign and continental newspapers are also sold in Old Compton Street by the upstarts, Capital Newsagents, adjoining Patisserie Valerie.

P. Denny and Co. Ltd (No. 39) has survived some hundred and twenty years, and is still fitting waiters and chefs with everything needed to wait and to chef; collars and cuffs, dickeys and ready-made bows, chefs' hats and table napkins. The window display in Frith Street is a wonderland. Coleman Cohens (No. 42) is the place for cigar-fanciers, and can do you cigars from fifteen countries. It has a continuously burning light on the counter as a courtesy to its customers. If pipes are your weakness, then Coleman Cohen's (a part of the national tobacconist chain, Findlay's, these days) can supply those too, but I strongly recommend bruyère, which is quite the best pipe-wood because it carbonises so satisfactorily. Pipes of a different complexion from Dreams of the Orient (No. 41B) – pipe-dreams evidently.

As to the English and Continental Pharmacie at No. 52, well, it's pleasant to see such a fine display of pharmaceuticalia, although a perfectly restored Victorian Chemists Shop is available for interested tourists a mile or two to the south in the Jersey Museum, St Helier. Three new developments in the street, Rushes, Marshall Cavendish and the Piccadilly Flower Company, while chic and prestigious in themselves, are disquieting, for their premises contain offices, and offices in Old Compton Street must be guarded against like the pest-house in Carnaby

Street. Always the charm of the area has been its smallness – in the basement a club, on the ground floor a shop, on the first floor a typist, on the top floor, well, anything is possible on the top floor! For Soho has so strong a sense of community, with hospitals and schools, ironmongers and wood workers, cream cakes and Peking ducks, film-moguls and bit-part players, that it remains special in a way that nowhere else in Central London is. Special, at least, to me. Indeed, the problem with Old Compton Street, a short and unpretentious road which is quite unnecessary as a thoroughfare (Shaftesbury Avenue joins Wardour Street and Charing Cross Road far more efficiently), is that there is far too much of interest in it. The improbably romantic but tragic story behind the resolutely shuttered Colombina d'Oro restaurant (No. 50) is not one I shall tell here – an invasion of private grief. And I will do no more than mention the excellent hair-cut I was given at Jim's (No. 7). Jim used to be at Cyril Henry (No. 41) but a hair transplant seems to have taken place. Cyril Henry, short, fat and round, is, according to Frankie Blake, good for a pound if you're skint.

As for the Prince Edward Theatre with its dauntingly monumental and sombre architecture – such a contrast with the glittering Buenos Aires presented within – it conceals quite a story. The interior design in fuchsia and gold with false fountains, diffused lighting, and Lalique glass panels, was based on the brave aesthetics of the Paris Exhibition of 1925; and much money was spent in providing the third-largest London theatre with every convenience, including sitting rooms for the star artistes. On 3 April 1930 the Prince Edward Theatre opened with *Rio Rita* (an ancestor of *Evita* evidently!), and was intended as a home for musical revue. But six years later the popularity of moving pictures caused it to be redesigned as the London Casino, a restaurant with provision for cabaret, dancing and films. Between 1940 and 1942 it closed out of deference to the V1s and V2s, after which it became a services club. In the utility years, glamorous escapism was a desperate requirement, and Robert Nesbitt provided it in 1949 with his silly, vulgar and inoffensive 'Latin Quarter' revue. Unable to choose between restaurant, theatre or cinema, the Casino was for twenty years from 1954 the home of Cinerama films. How thrilling it was in those innocent days to sit in one's seat and go down the bobsleigh run or the big dipper, ignoring, so far as it was possible, the misty lines where the pictures did not quite meet. With *Evita* in 1978 the building became once again a theatre and the title reverted to the name it was registered with at birth – the Prince Edward.

It is impossible to conclude this chapter without mentioning Old Compton Street's principal pre-occupation after food, the one which rears its ugly head, according to Noel Coward, 'when alligators thud through the Mississippi mud'. The Vice, as it is called, is on the decrease in Soho. In mid 1983, there were a hundred and sixty-four premises in the area given over to sex-related uses. By the end of 1984 seventy-one of those had closed down. There have been several changes, too, in the kind of services actually provided. Few bookshops and striptease clubs survive; indeed in the whole of Soho there are just three traditional strip-tease joints still in operation. The new fashion is for 'nude encounter studios' and 'peep-shows'. I cannot – no, to be honest I will not – report on the first, but peep-shows are dreadfully squalid, and several operate in Old Compton Street. You put your sticky fifty pence piece into a slot and a letter box falls open permitting you to gaze your fill into the private parts of some bored lady. Goodness knows what she thinks about as the poignant eyes peer at her: a bit like an unshelled lobster on a plate, I suspect. After maybe three minutes the letter box closes and a further investment is necessary if more gynaecological knowledge is to be gleaned. The good news is that these peep-shows have not been licensed and are therefore acting illegally. The bad news is that the low fines imposed by the magistrates and the lengthy delays at the Marlborough Street Court mean that the sex industry operators can profitably remain in business. Occasionally the police engage in detailed observation of some of the establishments from darkened windows opposite, but nothing seems to change as a result.

So far as book and video shops are concerned, a curious British compromise is currently being applied with the aproval (it seems) of most of the parties involved. These 'five percenter' shops are permitted to continue trading if they restrict their sexually explicit material to five per cent of their total stock. In Old Compton Street, Janus at No. 40 (a stylish early Victorian frontage) supplies magazines for those with a bent for bondage, and naughty schoolgirls, while Ann Summers opposite, behind its demurely lacy windows, offers a variety of sexual devices to boggle the imagination. I visited the old established Carnival Strip Club (No. 12) and found Rusty de Bono taking money (£4 a throw) at a small table, on which was a portable television and a pekinese. From time to time as we talked, the artistes would emerge, blinking, onto street level and hand Rusty their bets for Goodwood, featured that afternoon on his television. Obviously the going is tough at the Carnival on account of the clip joints. According to Rusty: 'By the time they get here they've spent all their money.' I can only imagine the pekinese was there to protect such money as punters have left to spend. I climbed down rickety stairs to what, even in the early days of fringe theatre, we would have considered sordid. The stage (about eight feet by four feet) was draped in indiscriminate shades of faded purple and scarlet. The set consisted of a large mirror stacked on the floor and a kitchen chair. The lighting – a colour wheel and an ultra violet strip; the special effects – one electric fan (working) for the audience; one electric fan (static) for the girls. I stayed for just two acts, a beautiful black girl and a beautiful white girl.

Both appeared initially in neglegées, both stripped off, spread their legs and toyed with themselves. They did their act to the Beatles, to Frankie Goes to Hollywood, two tracks to each act. The black girl's movements displayed a splendidly nonchalant arrogance. The white girl had shaved her pubes. As for the audience, which numbered twenty, they clustered in the front rows, leaping over the seats if one nearer the front became vacant. I would guess that the average age was the mid-fifties; the ones in the front row seemed older than the ones behind, almost as though they aged in their efforts to get to the front. Some seemed from the girls' reactions to be regulars, and they applauded appreciatively, almost, I thought, as if they were glad the act was over. I was reminded of Germaine Greer's amazement when she discovered just how deeply men hate women.

Although Old Compton Street has its share of derelicts, I saw no propositioning in the fresh air, but in Coral's betting-shop in Greek Street, a pretty blonde in mini-skirt picked up a successful punter and took him round the corner for a knee-trembler. There is no betting shop in Old Compton Street, and Coral's is the most adjacent. As betting shops go, it's quite adequate, with jovial counter ladies, and its clientele is predominantly West Indian. Years ago I was there when a fight broke out and knives flashed dangerously. I heard myself saying in my far back public school voice: 'I really wouldn't do that if I were you!' and the whole room exploded into loud laughter.

There is a generosity, it seems, in Soho, and even 'the Vice' seems scarcely serious. Perhaps this village atmosphere is what attracted many generations of Bohemians to it, so that even in the post-war years Bacon and Deacon and MacInnes, Driberg and Behan and Mulholland, Luard and Cook, Bernard and Taki, and many, many others would saunter from the French House to the Colony, from Wheeler's to the Mandrake, from Moroni's to the Marshall Street baths, taking pleasure in the time and the place, as, I'm sure, Henry Compton and Teresa Cornelys would have done.

3

St James's Street

The fishmonger, the orange-seller
and the wicked landlady

St James's Street, of classic fame!
   The finest people throng it! –
St James's Street? I know the name!
   I think I've passed along it!
Why, that's where Sacharissa sighed
   When Waller read his ditty;
Where Byron lived, and Gibbon died,
   And Alvanley was witty . . .

– *Frederick Locker-Lampson*

William Crockford was a fishmonger by trade. Physically repellent with fat white hands like filleted cod, he was born with one priceless asset – he had a fine head for figures. It was a useful talent for a fishmonger in Temple Bar, but when it came to laying the odds on Newmarket Heath, there was no one to come near him. Born in the 1770s, the story goes that he made his first pile in a marathon cribbage game at the Grapes in King Street, playing against the local champion, a butcher. Be that as it was, it was not too long before this deplorable, whey-faced, blubber-lipped, hump-backed, fish-smelling apology for a gentleman opened his first gambling club in St James's, followed in 1807 by his second, knocking down four mansions to create what is now the Jamaican High Commission two doors from Piccadilly. And on the night of the ninth of November, the Guards Club next door to the site of Crocky's new extravagance collapsed into the street, exposing to the vulgar gaze many of the Guards officers in their nightshirts. The reputations of some of them are supposed never to have recovered from that unprecedented exposure.

But what a club Crockford's was in those days! The fishmonger paid the great Eustache Ude, who had cooked for Louis XVI and the Buonaparte family, four thousand a year to create such masterpieces as his 'poudin de cerises à la Bentinck', and two thousand a year for dice. Membership of the club, which boasted the abstinent Duke of Well-

Left: The new face of St James's: offices at No. 66.

ington on the committee, was extremely hard to come by, but once you
were in, why then nothing could equal the splendour and excitement of
those glittering nights at Crockford's in the 1830's. Ude's creations, the
finest wines in the world and every luxury of the season, were all free, and
a most gentleman-like atmosphere prevailed. When Crockford died in
1844, and despite huge losses relating to his Newmarket piggeries and
another disastrous venture in St James's (the Bazaar, an early hyper-
market), the old boy was worth a quarter of a million pounds, with an
estate at racing's headquarters and a house in Carlton House Terrace
across the park from Her Majesty's residence (and putting *that* one to
shame, many believed).

Now the one thing which Crockford had never been able to achieve
was the status of a gentleman, and the only way he could realistically
expect to achieve it was to own the winner of the Derby. Many times he
had come close, but there had always been those – 'legs', jockeys, even
trainers – who had made it their business to see that his horses were
beaten. But the 1844 Derby offered him a superb chance in the handsome
thoroughbred form of Ratan. Other fancied entries included The Ugly
Buck, owned by Crockford's lifetime rival, the handsome John Gully,
ex-champion prize-fighter and respected MP; Leander, owned by the
continental Lichtwald Brothers; and Running Rein. The rumour goes
that three days before the running of the Derby, Crockford died. His
death would automatically have resulted in the scratching of his colt, so
its supporters propped Crockford up in his regular window wearing his
Nugee's surtout and faultless white cravat. If so, their cunning was
unrewarded. For arsenic had been administered to Ratan, who finished
seventh. The Ugly Buck was 'pulled' by his jockey, who may have been
acting under instructions from Crockford, while Leander's off-hind leg
was shattered on the hard going. So the race was won by Running Rein,
later disqualified, having been found to be a four-year-old 'ringer', in
favour of Colonel Peel's Orlando. In any event, the death of Crockford
marked the end of an era. Victorian London seemed vulgar and strait-
laced after the Regency excesses. Crockford's Club became a cheap
dining-house, where Irish buckeens, spring captains, welchers from the
ring, and suspicious-looking foreigners staggered up the gorgeous staircase, upon which the chivalry of England once loved to congregate.

Like it or lump it, that was, and still to some extent is, St James's
Street. A street of clubs. The real originals, not those pretentious piles
which mushroomed in Pall Mall. And, besides the clubs, a masculine
street where you could, and still can, buy hats and cigars and guns and
wine in shops with low ceilings and deferential servitors, who seem
themselves never to have had mothers (though possibly older, con-
scientious, spinster sisters). As soon as you reach Piccadilly all changes.
The *fin de siècle, beaux arts* Ritz is masculine enough outside with its

pompous arcade, but inside it is all gilded tables and shrill-voiced tourists from St Louis and Kentucky. And along Piccadilly paraded the ladies of the night. Piccadilly was originally Pickadilly, named after the Pickadil, or high ruffed collar, sold at 'Pickadilly Hall', a large establishment specialising in collar-making and tailoring. And in Piccadilly the old women of the Arts Council live and move and have their petits fours. In danger of becoming shrill myself, it may be wise to turn to the origins of this remarkable, handsome, and surprisingly steep street of St James. Surprisingly steep, because walking slowly or driving as fast as the traffic will allow northwards you don't notice the gradient, but there are those who claim that on a clear day from outside what was once Crockford's you can see to the Surrey Hills. Not that I've ever done it.

Henry Jermyn (1604–84), the Earl of St Albans, is generally considered by those who know about such things to have been the founder of London's West End. His father, Sir Thomas, had been a Privy Councillor and Vice-Chamberlain, but Henry had even more influence in the bedrooms of power as a result of his liaison with Henrietta Maria, the mother of the King. Some say he even married her, but what is certain is that in 1628 he was wittily appointed to be her Vice-Chamberlain. She must have been a remarkable woman because she forgave him readily for seducing one of her maids of honour (another witty signification); he certainly did not make the fatal mistake of marrying the unfortunate girl. In 1639 Henrietta Maria promoted Henry to be her Master of the House, in 1643 her Secretary and Colonel of her bodyguard, and finally handed over to him during the Commonwealth the complete management of her household. The King appointed him Lord High Admiral, for which he was perfectly qualified by having not the slightest interest in marine matters, and as a newly created Earl, he became English Ambassador in Paris. Here too he feathered his nest so that shortly after the Restoration this courtier with what Marwell described as 'drayman's shoulders and a butcher's mien' was able to buy a freehold of half, and a lease of the rest, of the forty-five acres known as St James's Fields. These fields ran north–south from Piccadilly to Pall Mall, and east–west from the Haymarket to St James's Street.

In the sixteenth century there had been little enough there except fields. St James's Palace is on the site of a leper hospital, or Lazarette. Piccadilly, an extension of Shaftesbury Avenue, was known as the 'way to Redinge' and there was a hedged lane of little consequence running from the one to the other. In St James's Square (or where that handsome square now stands) was a rotunda built of stone and a brick conduit. Francis Bacon wrote of both in *Historia Naturalis*: 'In the brick conduit there is a window and in the round house a slit or rift of some breadth . . . If you cry out in the rift it will make a fearful roaring at the window.'

We know that there were other buildings thereabouts because on 11 August 1556 Cromwell issued a proclamation forbidding further development in the area 'commonly called St James's Fields.' By 1559, if we accept the evidence of the rate books, there were just two residents of the street; a Mrs Anne Pulteney, the first of a long line of residents, and a Mr Baldwin, who in 1603 paid a pound in rates, and must consequently have owned an important property.

As the seventeenth century established itself, so too in St James's Street did a clutch of rich and fashionable personages, such as Sir Henry Henn (1619 though the knighthood came later), the Earl of Berkshire (1628), Sir Archibald Dowglass (1629), Lord Aston (1632), Sir W. Crofts (1634), Sir Ralph Chase (1635), and Sir John Bingley, afterwards Lord Andover (1636). During the 1640s two earls, a countess, five lords, a lady, three knights, and Captain Scares, 'who pays six shillings for a garden' and built a garden-house for 'old Perkins', joined their company.

In 1661-2 the street was paved by order of the King, and acquired the name it bears today. It had been known – but it's hard to imagine why – as the Long Street.

In 1644 a water-supply was installed, using 'an engine which by perpetual motion will drain level or mines, though fifty fathoms deep'. It is a curiosity that one of the commissioners responsible for ordering the street to be improved was the diarist, John Evelyn, who regarded it as little better than a quagmire, though obviously a busy one. And by 1667 there were thirty-nine names on the register including Lady Pike, Sir John Fenwick and Lady Burlard, who each paid £2 in rates, and the well-heeled Lady Scrope, who paid £3.

Obviously such rate-payers were not just rich but influential, for in 1665 the St James's Fair had become such a nuisance to people of breeding that it was moved elsewhere, finding a home at last on 'the road leading to Tyburn' (the present Park Lane, as near as makes no odds) and giving the name Mayfair to that region which, in the minds of John Waddingtons, is the most fanciable in London (a hotel on Mayfair – £2,000!).

Now the Earl really got to work, and, around a central piazza (St James's Square, a notable venue for duellists) and in collaboration with Sir Thomas Clarges, doctor, courtier, financier, started a massive speculative development. So in 1667 came Jermyn Street, named modestly after himself, and King Street in 1673, named tactfully after his patron. The rest followed with Wren's church of St James's, regarded by the architect as his best design for a Parish Church, to supply the spiritual needs of those whose temporal affairs were in good shape (with the possible exception of a Mr Richardson who would not pay his rates and subsequently disappears from the records). It is worth remarking that Wren designed St James's to face Jermyn Street, not Piccadilly.

However fashionable St James's Street became in the late seventeenth century, it was the houses along the southern side of Pall Mall, with their views across the park, which were regarded as the most desirable. Here lived the Countess of Ranelagh whose husband 'spent more money, built more fine houses, and laid out more on household furnishing and gardening than any other Nobleman in England'. Also Nell Gwynn who could (and did) chat to the King across the garden wall from No. 79. Nell was a practical girl and, when the King gave her a leasehold (for the house belonged to him), she returned it announcing that she had always offered her services free under the Crown and expected the Crown to do the same for her! It did, and No. 79 has been private property ever since. So too is Schomberg House, one of the few surviving (though restored) examples of a London house of that period; Gainsborough lived and died there. And, of course, in Marlborough House lived Sarah, the Duchess.

But St James's Street had another and more violent aspect. There was a nasty incident in 1674 when the Duke of Ormond was waylaid by five or more highwaymen, but boldly disarmed one of them and scared off the rest, being left with bruises and cuts to the head and a bald-faced chestnut horse which the villains left behind. The street also housed James Maclean, the gentleman highwayman. It was a hotbed of Jacobite sedition, and in the numerous taverns and coffee and chocolate houses there were many lowered voices and averted eyes. On the death of Queen Anne, Atterbury offered to go down in front of St James's in full episcopal robes and proclaim King James III, and rash Mr Ozinda of Ozinda's Chocolate House was led away captive, along with two other loyal habitués, Captain Forde and Sir Richard Vivyan. Captain Gronow was a witness to Corn Law riots in St James's, when the Life Guards were stoned to a chorus of 'down with the Piccadilly butchers' and there was even a riot (though not much of a one) in St James's Street in the 1880s when the Fair Trade League, an organisation of unemployed men, met a counter organisation, known as the Social-Democratic Federation (that has a familiar ring to it!) outside the Reform Club the servants of that august institution throwing old nail-brushes, shoes and other unwanted impedimenta down upon the warring factions.

But to return to the seventeenth century. Blind and senile, the old Earl of St Albans left the development of the north of the street to others younger and more energetic. The Earl of Arlington sold a plot to a Mr Pym, who built a number of houses which were so badly contructed that they fell down again almost at once. A certain Charles Godolphin in St James's Place was so infuriated to find an MP, Thomas Coke, building a house slap up against his property that he cocked his pistol and threatened to shoot any workman whose head appeared in view above his garden wall. The Earl of Clarendon built a huge pile to the north of Piccadilly but chose exile in preference to impeachment for high treason, and the mansion was sold at half its cost to the feckless Duke of Albermarle and then to a group of speculators headed by Sir Thomas Bond. You will, of course, recognise many street names associated with these courtiers and developers. Others were Berkeley Street (after Berkeley House, built in 1664 by Lord Berkeley of Stratton) and Burlington Gardens (after Burlington House, built between 1663 and 1668 by the Earl of Cork and Burlington).

At this time there were many courts opening out of St James's Street: Villiers Court, Crown and Sceptre Court, Fox Court, Gloucester Court and Pickering Place to the east, and Stable Yard, Little St James's Street, and Thatched House Court to the west. Of these the delightful Pickering Place and Little St James's Street survive, at least in part. Pickering Place was once the site of the Hell Hole, a notorious gaming house and brothel. The rather ugly stone bust to be seen in Pickering Place is a representation of Lord Palmerston which an antique shop threw out and the dustmen refused to take away.

Besides chocolate and coffee houses, there were several taverns including The Cock, The King's Head and The Poet's Head (probably with a sign depicting Dryden), the Horse Shoe Ale House and The Bunch of Grapes, which advertised in 1711 its 'extraordinary good cask Florence wine at six shillings a gallon'.

By the mid eighteenth century, if we judge by Rocque's famous map, the Street was, at least in its broad outlines, much as today. But in 1765 a revolutionary idea was put into practice – the steep gradients of St James's Street were levelled with results which had not been anticipated. A letter to the *London Chronicle* (15 August 1765) is worth quoting at length.

> . . . some of the ground floors, that were almost level with the street, are now eight, nine, and some ten steps, and those very steep from the ground; while others, to which you used to ascend by three or four steps, are now as many below the surface. Cellars are now above ground and some gentlemen are forced to dive into their own parlours. Many laughable accidents have happened from this new method of turning the world upside down. Some persons, not thinking of the latter alterations, attempting to knock at their own door, have frequently tumbled up their new-erected steps, while others, who have been used to ascent to their threshold, have as often, for the same reason, tumbled down and their fall had been greater, from their lifting up their legs to ascend as usual. An old gouty friend of mine complains heavily; he has lain, he says, upon the ground floor for these ten years, and he chose the house he lives in because there was no step to the door; and now he is obliged to mount at least nine before he can

Right: Pickering Place, a court out of St James's.

get into his bedchamber . . . A neighbour, too, complains he has lost a good lodger, because he refused to lower the price of his first floor, which the gentleman insisted he ought, as the lodgings are now up two pair of stairs. Many of the street doors are not above five foot high; and the owners when they enter their houses, seem as if they were going into a dog kennel, rather than their own habitations. To say the truth, no fault can be imparted to the trustees: but many are great sufferers; and this method of making the houses conform to the ornamental paving, is something like the practice of Procrustes, the robber, who made a bed of certain dimensions, and whoever was put into it, had his legs cut shorter if they were too long, or stretched out if they were too short, till the poor wretch was precisely of the length with the bed.

I am, Sir, Yours & etc
'Anti-Procrustes'.

While on the subject of lodging-house keepers in St James's, I cannot resist mentioning the dreaded Mrs Trifoli of Duke Street whom Mrs Letitia Pilkington (1712–50) refers to in her memoirs thus:

A most extraordinary painted up, wizened out old woman, whose husband was a German quack, not then in England, from which, it seems his wife had obliged him to fly, for robbing her of a deed of settlement he had made on her at marriage; but to say the truth, I think that was a blessing on the poor man, for she was a very Devil-incarnate, unmerciful and cruel to the last degree . . . Her custom was to live upon her lodgers, even when she knew they were desolately poor, in so much that, if one of them sent but for a pint of small beer, she would intercept it in the way and drink half of it; but indeed she was very civil, for she always sent them word she drank their health, and so she did in reality, yea, their very vital blood.

(This anecdote recalls to my mind my time as a washer-up at Butlin's Clacton Camp in the 1950s. The campers' tables were numbered, and a huge clock at the end of the dining hall was spun each evening to indicate the winning table. Its occupants won a bottle of something like champagne, but were encouraged by redcoats to drink Billy Butlin's health with it.)

The oldest club in St James's is White's Club (No. 37), which evolved in 1693 from a coffee house of the same name. It was renowned as a hotbed of the Tory establishment (if that isn't a contradiction in terms), and its principal St James's Street rivals were Brooks's, Boodle's, Almack's and, of course, Crockford's. A Yorkshireman, William Almack, once a valet, later a coffee-house keeper, made so much money out of his investment in Brooks's that he was able to open his own club, Almack's, in 1765, and this celebrated establishment quickly came to

Brooks's Club.

rival Mrs Cornelys's (see the chapter on Old Compton Street). Incidentally, Almack's real name was Macall, but he anagrammatised it (more or less). Lady Pembroke was his associate in the enterprise. What was novel about Almack's was that it was a club for *both* sexes, in which the women nominated and voted for the men, and vice versa. The results of the voting were consequently intriguing. Even the Duchess of Bedford was blackballed when she first applied. Parties were held weekly for a three-month season, for which the subscription was ten guineas, including all the supper you could eat. The appeal of the club was to the younger element. Horace Walpole was a member:

'I am afraid to say I am of so young and fashionable society: but as they are people I live with, I choose to be idle rather than morose. I cannot go to a younger supper without forgetting how much sand is run out of the hourglass.'

As with most of the clubs, gambling was all-important, and at Almack's stakes were high. Every player was required to have at least 30 guineas on the table and it was commonplace for ten thousand pounds in gold to be visible on the green baize. To play, the participants either removed their coats or turned them inside out for luck, putting on leather brassards to protect their lace cuffs, and wearing high-crowned straw hats decorated with flowers and ribbons to shade their eyes. They might also wear face-masks to conceal their emotions.

As Austin Dobson put it:

> The ladies of St James's
>   Wear satin on their backs;
> They sit all night at Ombre,
>   With candles all of wax;
> But Phyllida, my Phyllida!
>   She dons her russet gowns,
> And runs to gather May dew
>   Before the world is down.

It is certainly my view that life with the ladies of St James's would be more fun than with russet-gowned Phyllida. (In other verses we learn that Phyllida wears buckled shoon, no make-up, and goes courting beneath the harvest moon – which implies not very often, I suppose.)

The men's clubs, White's and Brooks's and Boodle's, survived where the livelier halls did not, and those who go in search of a wild time have not patronised for well over a hundred years, and probably will not patronise for a hundred years to come, St James's Street. The atmosphere of these clubs has not changed much and will probably continue not to change much. 'Stuffy' is the apposite adjective, but this is stuffiness carried to a fine art, it is stuffiness *per se*. Arnold Bennett, who was extremely clubbable, still had the wit to describe such places well. This is a typical smoking room at night:

> The atmosphere of the place has put . . . them into a sort of exquisite coma. Their physical desires are assuaged, and they know by proof that they are in charge of the most perfectly organised mechanism of comfort that was ever devised . . . They know that never an Oriental despot was served better than they . . . In comparison, the most select hotels and restaurants are a hurly-burly of crude socialism. The bell is under the hand, and the labelled menial stands with everlasting patience near; and home and women are far away.

A roster of the principal St James's Street clubs runs as follows: Brook's (No. 60) named after a wine merchant and money-lender for country gentlemen; White's (No. 37); Boodle's (No. 28) for country gentlemen; the Carlton (Nos. 69–70); the Bath or Conservative Club (No. 74); and the Royal Ocean Yacht Club (No. 20). The St James's Club and the Royal Overseas League are in Park Place. The Carlton moved to St James's after its Pall Mall premises were bombed in 1940. I realise, just in time, that I have said nothing about the one thing not even a tourist can miss in St James's Street, which is the Palace. I mentioned only that it had been an asylum for lepers, 'for maidens that were lepers living chastely and honestly in divine service', if I am to be quite accurate; but on the site of this sad place Henry VIII built a royal palace, perhaps to the designs of Holbein. It has been rather an insulted sort of palace, for although Charles II, James II, Mary, and Queen Anne were born here, all prefered to live at Whitehall Palace, burned down in 1698. Queen Victoria took the Court to Buckingham Palace in 1837, so it was only properly a Hanoverian Residence. Charles Dickens explains the reasons for the Palace's royal disfavour thus: 'Of late years its cramped and inconvenient rooms have been found highly impracticable . . . and Her Majesty's drawing rooms have been removed to Buckingham Palace, where the fight for priority of admission to the royal presence is not embittered by quite such close packing, and Her Majesty's lieges are enabled to preserve their toilettes on comparatively sound condition even to the exit'. But the Gentlemen of Arms and the Yeomen of the Guard have their headquarters here, and foreign ambassadors are accredited to the Court of St James's, not the newly arrived Buckingham Palace. The musical tradition at St James's Palace is superb, for it counts amongst its choristers and organists Tallis, Byr, John Bull, Orlando Gibbons, Purcell, Boyce and Sullivan.

Another distinction is that it is hugely haunted. Sellis, the Duke of Cumberland's Italian valet, sits up in bed, his throat cut by his master from ear to ear. Before murdering his valet, the wicked Ernest had impregnated his valet's daughter, who killed herself from shame. George III's fifth son was so unpopular thereafter that he was booed in public. Not only may the blood-drenched valet be seen from time to time, but the ghostly smell of his blood hangs in the air.

Then there is the curious tale of two royal mistresses, narrated in Peter Underwood's splendid volume *Haunted London* (Harrap, 1973). Charles II's mistress, the Duchess of Mazarin, and Charles's brother James II's mistress, Madame de Beauclair, were intimates and had suites in the Palace. In retirement, they discussed weighty matters, such as the immortality of the soul, and agreed that whichever predeceased the other should pay a return visit to her friend. When the Duchess of Mazarin was dying, she reaffirmed this promise in front of witnesses.

Fifteen years passed and Madame de Beauclair had received no visitation. Surely this must mean that there was no such thing as immortality. But one night a friend received an urgent summons to St James's Palace if she wanted to see Madame Beauclair alive. An even more urgent summons was accompanied by a casket of jewels as a bribe. Arriving at the palace, Mme de Beauclair's friend was surprised to find her looking fit and well, but apparently she was about to die. She had received a visit from the Duchess, who had made a circuit of the bed 'swimming rather than walking', and, stopping beside an Indian chest, had said 'with her usual sweetness': 'Between the hours of twelve and one tonight you will be with me'. Sure enough, just as the clock began striking midnight, Mme de Beauclair gasped: 'Oh, I am sick at heart!' and, thirty minutes later, expired.

Other neighbourhood ghosts include the headless woman in St James's Park and the ghost of an old dresser who haunted the lovely old St James's Theatre in King Street, which was replaced with offices in 1957 by developers who perhaps are haunted through the long watches of the night by their own vandalism. For the record, the offices are now leased by the Dunlop Rubber Company. The theatre, though charming, had a serious drawback in the pillars which ruined the sight-lines from many seats in the stalls. The theatre had been notable since 1835 for undemanding fare, and was where you would go to see Pinero's plays interpreted by that matinée idol, Sir George Alexander, whose following was strongest amongst fashionable ladies with cut-glass accents. In 1893 the theatre had been the home for a more controversial success: *The Second Mrs Tanqueray.*

If you still have the nerve to visit St James's Palace, be warned that the state apartments are not open to the public, though Ambassadors Court is, as are the services in the Chapel Royal with its marvellous coffered ceiling, supposedly by Holbein. In the Chapel Royal Charles I prayed; half an hour later his head was cut off. You can worship on Sundays (8.30 and 11.15 a.m.) from October to Palm Sunday, and on Good Friday. If you visit the choral service (11.30) on 6 January, the Feast of Epiphany, royal gifts of gold and frankincense and myrrh are offered up. Equally worth a visit is Lancaster House, which, with the less distinguished Clarence House, completes the royal complex. Lancaster House, which is open all week-ends and bank holidays from 2 p.m. to 6 p.m., from Easter to mid-December, is very grand and ideal for state banquets. It has a marvellous staircase in the Italian taste and a Great Gallery no less than one hundred and twenty feet long.

It was to St James's Palace that I went to have my play *The Fourth of June* censored. Brigadier Gwatkin represented the Lord Chamberlain in this matter, and had much to tell us about what 'the man upstairs' would or would not permit. Finally I inquired about the mysterious requirement

St James's Palace.

that 'the name Lady Pinkus shall be deleted wherever it occurs'. 'Why?' I asked the Brigadier, who, wagging a military finger at me, replied: 'You can't fool us, you know. Pink arse! Pink arse!'

In St James's Street today one can see in dramatic confrontation the antique and the hypermodern. Surviving from the eighteenth century are several wonderful shop-fronts, while modernism is displayed in the offices of *The Economist* and the Plaza in front of it, set back a little from the road and successfully designed by Alison and Peter Smithson in 1966; and the recently completed offices at No. 66, in futuristic rocket-launcher style of granite, grey steel and curved glass – design by Tripos. The Economist Plaza is to be seen as directly in line of descent from the seventeenth-century courts while, distorted in the windows of No. 66 – a pastiche, perhaps deliberate, of the traditional bow windows of the clubs – may be seen reflections of the eighteenth century.

The shops are wonderful of course. Lock & Co, Hatters, at No. 6, is at least two hundred and fifty years old. Here was created the first bowler, except that Lock's have always called it a Coke, in honour of William Coke, gentleman of Leicester, who wanted a suitable hat for his gamekeepers. The material for the Coke was supplied by Messrs Bowler. At Lock's they take an impression of the head of each new customer, so

Lock & Co., Hatters.

that future requirements may be easily supplied. The Earl of Rosebery
used merely to stand in the doorway and shout: 'Hat!' Here tricorns
(displayed in the window) were sold to Nelson and Brummel, and since
Conan Doyle was hatted at Lock's, one can safely assume that Sherlock
Holmes would have bought his deer-stalker there. Here recently I saw in
the window a pith helmet for sale. Once upon a time, black silk hats
would be returned to Lock's in the spring to be 'Dressed, Lined and
Bound' in time for Royal Ascot. 'Drab Shells', grey toppers that is, are far
more recent vulgarities. Kaye Webb told a story of a military gentleman
who would kneel down in church each Sunday with his top-hat in front
of his face. 'Why?' asked a companion. The reply: 'I say "James Lock &

Lobb's in St James's

Co, Hatters, 6 St James's Street, London SW1" into it three times; then I know it's all right to get up!'

Records at Lock's suggest that Englishmen's heads are growing significantly larger all the time. I have no records, however, relating to the heads of other nations.

At No. 9, John Lobb's is the oldest surviving bootmaker in London. There may be seen the last made for Queen Victoria's shoes, and each serious customer will merit a personal last. If you wish to buy your boots and shoes at Lobb's, you should be both rich and patient, an unusual combination.

The original John Lobb lived an eventful and romantic life. Crippled as a child in Fowey, Cornwall, he limped the long trek to London with the ambition of finding work at Thomas's of St James's, the leading bootmaker of the day. But he was not wanted there, so he sailed for Australia where the gold-rush was at its height, and by making boots for the prospectors and marrying the daughter of Sydney's harbour-master, he became both rich and celebrated. He returned to England and won a gold medal at the 1862 Exhibition, the first of many such medals. He also acquired a Warrant from the Prince of Wales by the mere device of sending him a beautifully crafted pair of boots to fit the Prince's feet. Helped by the generosity of John Lewis, Lobb opened a shop in Regent Street before moving to St James's, to drive Thomas's out of business – a long anticipated revenge. The present premises at No. 9, St James's Street are not antique, though they appear to be, but a clever artifice. Within is a library of twenty thousand lasts, each made specifically to fit a customer's feet. When in 1956 Charles Morgan was sent by the *Daily Mail* to interview the gravely ill Max Beerbohm in Rapallo, the Grand old man opened the conversation by inquiring: 'Tell me, is Lobb still the best bootmaker in London?'

St James's Street was also the home of another, and in his time even more famous, bootmaker. Hoby supplied Wellington with his boots. He did more. He claimed to have won all his battles for him by making his boots and praying for him in Islington (Hoby was also a Methodist preacher). E. V. Lucas recalls a splendid occasion, which gives us some idea of the quality of the man. A certain Horace Churchill, Ensign in the Guards, having exclaimed in a passion that he would never buy boots at Hoby's again, Hoby called quietly to an assistant in the shop: 'John, put up the shutters. It's all over with us. Ensign Churchill has withdrawn his custom!'

No. 19 is one of two celebrated cigar shops in St James's Street (the other is Davidof at No. 35). Robert Lewis has cigars floor to ceiling, more than a quarter of a million of them, in the humidified air. For sixty-four years Churchill had an account at the shop, from which he obtained his favourites: hand-rolled Romeo y Julietas. His secretary wrote to the shop once ordering a box of twenty-five cigars for his grandson's birthday, specifying: 'Not quite as good as the Romeo y Julieta'. Havanas are the shop's speciality, but their longest cigar is a Jamaican at a full twelve-inch.

To complement your cigars from Davidof or Robert Lewis, you will need port and this may be ordered from either Justerini and Brooks (No. 61) or Berry Bros. and Rudd (No. 3), a shop dating back to 1730 and scarcely changed. It has cellars extending far below the street. At Berry Bros. Lord Byron (who woke up one morning in 1811 at No. 8 St James's Street to find himself famous) and Tom Moore would buy their port, possibly something akin to the Special Reserve, Superlative Old Tawny,

The cellars of Berry Bros.

which is not flattered by its description. And this building too was the site of the Texan Legation to the Court of St James's between 1842 and 1845.

Berry Brothers and Rudd opened its doors in the 1690s as an Italian grocer, selling wine, tea and coffee. The tea and coffee arrived in sacks and the sacks were weighed in a large set of scales. In 1765 a unique tradition was initiated when Berry's began also to weigh their customers. There were no such things as bathroom scales, of course, and many St James's clubmen did need to watch their figures.

Fortunately, records of these weigh-ins have survived, and we can see how much such customers as Pitt, Beaux Nash and Brummell, Prinny and Byron weighed. Some were so alarmed at what they saw that they insisted that the records add 'wearing heavy top-coat'! In the present century Rosa Lewis and the Aga Khan (grandfather of the present Aga) were regulars in the scales. Usually customers bought a case of wine while being weighed, so business boomed.

To protect your wine and cigars from predators you will need to visit either Chubb Security at No. 69, another fine old shop front with windows framed by columns of blue and white barley sugar twist, but what the windows reveal are hideous promotional displays and an office furnished with mind-boggling banality; or, in extremis, William Evans, gun and rifle manufacturers. Another fine shop; another disquieting window display. Despite the sign affirming that the shop is a Game Conservancy Member, most of the goods relate to destruction rather than conservancy. Inside William Evans is a formidable array of sporting guns in racks, a green-shaded aneucapnic lamp hanging beneath a brass ventilating fan, shooting sticks erect, and a desk laid out with gun-cleaning equipment. The over-riding impression is of mahogany and brass, and the grim and expensive business of killing small mammals and birds. Amongst other items I noted dog whistles, 'sonic-hearing protectors', beautifully made wooden cases of gun-cleaning equipment, travelling bridge sets, flasks, mittens, cravats, dog-leads, pouches, William Evans brand cartridges, and guns, guns, guns. It's a relief to visit Harris, the old-fashioned chemist at No. 30, by appointment to the Queen Mother who lives, of course, just down the road at Clarence House. Here you (and maybe Her Majesty) can buy their Original Pick Me Up in its modest green bottle. 'This celebrated preparation has during the last 60 years received the most distinguished patronage of the English and foreign courts. One tablespoon in a wine glass of water occasionally.' It would, of course, be a wine glass! Also for sale are bristle brushes, sponges, Arlington toilet-waters for men and 'Witch' roll-on deodorants for women, and all the rest of the chemists' stock-in-trade. (Other splendid toiletries may be found in Jermyn Street.)

Almost in St James's Street is Christie's, the auctioneers, at No. 8 King's Street. James Christie was a Perth man. Born in 1730, he worked in various London auction houses having retired from the Navy. He was a man 'of tall and dignified appearance, remarkable for eloquence, and professional enthusiasm'. He also kept a fine table, serving venison and claret to an entourage known as 'Christie's Fraternity of Godfathers'. As was politic for a dealer in pictures (which is principally what Christie sold in the early days), he counted Gainsborough, Reynolds, and Richard Wilson among his friends. Once he stood security for a young man's debts (amounting, some say, to £20,000) and the young man died before reaching his majority, so that Christie lost the entire sum. He was saved in this calamity by David Garrick, the actor, who made him a generous loan until he was back on his feet. After Garrick died, his widow gave Christie the actor's effects to sell, and Christie from the rostrum told the buyers of Garrick's generosity. The auctioneer was succeeded by his son, and the old place – very elegant it is too – still has very much the air of an establishment for Regency gentlemen of leisure. Auction houses survive longer than other establishments. Still in business in London are Phillips, Sotheby's and Bonham's, all over a century old.

As you would expect for so masculine a street, St James's is well-supplied with eating, drinking, and accommodating establishments. Rosa Lewis, of course, the notorious Duchess of Duke Street, ran the most accommodating – the Cavendish Hotel in Jermyn Street, with a back entrance in Duke Street – as an eccentric if disreputable port of call. A marvellous cook herself, she believed that Englishwomen could be the best cooks in the world.

Rosa Lewis was the daughter of an undertaker and worked herself up from being a menial domestic servant to the prestigious position of cook to Lady Randolph Churchill. After a marriage of convenience to a society butler, Rosa moved to Eaton Square where her house, No. 55, was a convenient place for the Prince of Wales, among others, to further his liaisons. Meanwhile she was pursuing a successful career, catering to the gentry. In 1902 she bought the Cavendish Hotel, which was both fashionable and louche. It was a most convenient establishment for the clubmen of St James's, who could wine and dine their particular friends with no questions asked.

In the rebuilt Cavendish Hotel portraits of Rosa overhang the staircase and the downstairs bar is naughtily entitled Sub Rosa. Also in the hotel are typical Rosa menus and a framed cheque for 'one billion pounds – thick gold pounds' made out to Bearer and signed by Rosa Lewis. Rosa was characterised as Lottie Crump in Evelyn Waugh's *Vile Bodies,* and on television as *The Duchess of Duke Street.*

Next door to the Cavendish there used to be a Turkish bath in which, even in the early sixties, young men could spend an inexpensive and comfortable night drying out. I did so myself once. A newspaper would be brought to you with your breakfast, and the towels were long and thick. A curiosity of the place was that the cubicles were anything but sound-proofed. I heard a cad telling a friend that he had married a Windmill girl. Was it working out, the friend wanted to know. 'Not really,' said the other. What he hadn't known when he married her was that she would bruise so easily . . .

Also closed, though quite recently, and sorely missed, is Madame Prunier's establishment, opened as an extension of the Paris fish-restaurant, but restaurants in St James's have to struggle to co-exist with the clubs, and since the St James's Theatre closed there is really no reason why anyone should need to eat there at nights. What used to be Prunier's is now the Sun Tory on the corner of Little St James's Street, an upmarket Japanese restaurant, specialising in Teppan cooking. This is cooking on an iron plate set into the top of the table, which is, apparently, how they eat in Osaka. The windows are tastefully set with decorative wood and pottery and pussy-willow, and a menu indicating that you will need to be rich to eat Osaka style. Prices range from the Matsu Course (£14.95) to the Imperial Teppan-Yaki Course (£23) with a 15% service charge and Pouilly Fuissé 1983 at £17.25 per bottle. The only other restaurant actually in St James's is the old-fashioned Overton's (No. 5), notable once for its oysters and deferential waiters, but unexceptional these days. Several restaurants and catering pubs in the neighbourhood survive to service the rumbling tummies of journalists from *The Economist*, or hungry insurance executives from the Norwich Union, the Scottish Union, the Abbey National and the Sun Alliance, and beautifully restored picture dealers from Noortman and Brod. Green's Champagne and Oyster Bar (36 Duke Street) has revived the art of the great British pudding and serves Spotted Dick, Treacle Sponge, Jam Roly Poly, and Bakewell or Treacle Tart, though not all on the same day. Fishcakes, steak and kidney pudding, boiled beef and dumpling, pigeon pie and, of course, oysters provide equally splendid British grub. I wonder if the Sun Tory waiters ever try jam roly poly, and, if so, what they think of it!

As for pubs, I suggest The Golden Lion (25 King Street) which serves excellent lunches and Burton Ale and Best Bitter from hand-pumps. The most privileged seat is the back cabinet of the downstairs bar – rather nice. The Red Lion (2 Duke Street) is dreadfully crowded during the rush hours, but has wonderfully engraved glass, like a fantasy hall of mirrors. Each mirror depicts a British flower.

This then is St James's Street; once steep, now levelled; once raucous, now staid; mainly for men. Boots, hats, wine, cigars, the guardsmen outside St James's Palace, the club members snoozing over their port. It's not what it was! The Map Shop, Madame Prunier's, Almack's, Crockford's, The Devonshire, even the British Tourist Board and the Post Office – gone, all gone. It is a piece of old London with a pace-maker instead of a heart. It has seen the best of its time. No wonder the ghosts haunt it so energetically.

4

Whitechapel Road

Milk, mosques and penny gaffs

Pumbedita, Cordova, Cracow, Amsterdam,
  Vilna, Lublin, Berditchev and Volozhin,
Your names will always be sacred
  Places where Jews have been.

And sacred is Whitechapel,
  It is numbered with our Jewish towns.
Holy, holy, holy
  Are your bombed stones.

If we ever have to leave Whitechapel
  As other Jewish towns were left,
Its soul will remain a part of us,
  Woven into us, woof and weft.

– *Avram Stencl*

It was not an evening like other evenings. We had been to see the fey
Lindsay Kemp in his phantasmagoric performance of Jean Genet's
Flowers. Then walking down the Whitechapel Road there loomed in
front of us a mosque, looking like a cardboard assembly, and one which I
never remembered having seen before, lighted from within, and behind
its minaret a crescent moon, vulgar in its perfection. From the mosque
poured a babble of young muslim boys in white caps, for it was the feast of
Shab-e-Barat. Outside the mosque souvenirs and sweetmeats were being
sold. An atmosphere of festivity was all-pervasive. Later we spotted a
group of Muslim boys walking home across the deserted churchyard of St
Mary Matfelon, the crescent moon still grinning down as mysterious as
the Cheshire Cat. Later still, walking along the river bank at Ham-
mersmith Mall, we saw that the moon was now perfectly round, as
complete as an unskinned orange, and no clouds anywhere in the sky.

The following week-end a small item in the *Observer* drew the attention of curious readers to the unusual event of a total eclipse of the moon
which had taken place a few nights previously. But we knew better. It was
Lindsay Kemp and the power of prayer that had done it, just as Joshua
had made the sun stand still.

Whitechapel Road Mosque.

Whitechapel is the place for miracles. Horrors too. It has played host to the Huguenots, the Irish and the Jews, the Greek Cypriots, the Maltese and the Pakistanis, to Doctor Barnardo and to Jack the Ripper.

In 1751 a pony trotted thirty miles out from Whitechapel Church and back again in ten hours and thirty-one minutes, winning a wager of fifty guineas for its owner with twenty-nine minutes in hand. In 1742 in a vault under St Botolph's, Aldgate, was found the body of a boy, aged about 12 and perfectly preserved, which had been walled up during the Great Plague of 1665. One Saturday morning in 1829, the coachman employed by Joseph Tickell, brewer, of Whitechapel, was expressing his partiality for a favourite horse by kissing it (and why not?) when the animal suddenly bit off the coachman's under-lip and swallowed it. Miracles and horrors. The miracles sometimes resulting from the horrors. No part of London could show such squalour as could be found in Old Montague Street, the Ratcliff Highway, or The Old Nichol (Arthur Morrison's Jago). Here is a contemporary account (or as much as I can stomach!) of 1827:

> In Whitechapel, the putrid mixture of gore and excrementitious matters proceeding from the animals slaughtered there, instead of passing into the common sewer, is daily disposed over the whole surface of that wide street, in place of pure water, which in all other parts of the metropolis is used! The putrefying miasmata exhaled from this under the influence of a scorching sun, and wafted down the close and narrow lanes by the sultry breezes of summer, is, and must be, a most productive cause of typhus fever, and other putrid diseases as they are termed, which at this season abound in that neighbourhood. Were human ingenuity taxed to compound a malaria of concentrated power, none more deadly could be imagined.

And yet it was in this miasma of Whitechapel that philanthropists, writers, and social reformers wrought their miracles. Canon and Mrs Barnett, William Booth, Octavia Hill, Angela Burdett-Coutts, Walter Besant, Arnold Toynbee, Arthur Morrison, Dean Champneys, William Davis, Dr Barnardo, Basil Henriques, Samuel Montagu, Israel Zangwill, Charles Booth, and Mrs Webb, all were from, of, or for the East End.

A brief history of the area: in the Domesday Book the East End was contained within the Manor of Stibenhede (Stepney), and clustered around the ancient church of St Dunstan and All Saints. A Saxon cross in the Apse is a relic of the original church founded by Dunstan, Bishop of London, in 952. Once this church was the site of a primitive parliament. One vicar, Richard Fox, was to baptise Henry VIII. Another was John Colet, intimate of Erasmus and Thomas More, and later Dean of St Paul's. The present church in Kentish ragstone survived the blitz and boasts a magnificent east window (by Hugh Easton) which celebrates Christ resurrected above the bombed ruins of Stepney.

In the fourteenth century invalids visited St Mary's Spital for its sweet, fresh country air, and St Leonard's, Shoreditch, was harmoniously set amidst gardens and fruit trees. The City Hunt had its kennels there, there were ponds to bathe and fish in with cattle grazing in pasture rich with Roman remains. The East End began (or terminated) at the old Roman Wall, twenty-two feet high, with Aldgate, a massive double-entrance, on the outer towers of which the heads of criminals were ominously displayed. Outside the gates lay The Hermitage, inhabited by mendicants, and close by was St Mary's, a white chapel of ease, built about 1270, from which Whitechapel derived its name. On this site

A general view of Whitechapel Road.

churches came and went, five in all, until the Germans destroyed the last one during the war to end all wars. To be quite accurate, the 1940 air raid destroyed all but the tower and spire of the church and a fragment of nave wall. In 1945 the spire was struck by lightning and what remained had to be demolished. Also destroyed was one of London's few open-air pulpits. The churchyard is still in evidence, and a drinking fountain erected in 1860 'by one unknown, yet well known', but this gives no water. If Aldgate formed the western extremity to Whitechapel, then to the east it terminated at Mile End where there was a toll-gate. In 1866 all London toll-gates were abolished by Act of Parliament and the last Mile End gate-keeper was forced by an over-enthusiastic crowd, celebrating the end of such restraints, to take to his heels and flee top-hat in hand, from a fate which might have involved dirty water, since there was also in Whitechapel a ducking-pond (near Brady Street); this was used, we learn, 'for curing shrewish wives, drunkards, and other obnoxious persons'.

It was during the sixteenth century that Whitechapel's character changed significantly from open countryside to slum. Mile End Green was common land but John Stow, writing at that time, complained that the beauty of the Essex Road, was being 'encroached upon by the building of filthy cottages . . . that in some places it scarce remaineth a sufficient highway for the meeting of carriages and droves of cattle. Much less is there any fair, pleasant or wholesome way for people to walk on foot, which is no small blemish to so famous a city to have so unsavoury and unseemly an entrance to it.' The road was paved in 1542.

To the south of the main road there had been an abbey (dissolved in the 1530s) belonging to the nuns of the Order of St Clare, the sisters being known as Minoresses and the area therefore the Minories. In a celebrated passage John Stow remembers when as a boy he used to visit a farm belonging to the nuns, 'at the which farm I myself in my youth have fetched many a halfpenny worth of milk, and never had less than three ale pints for a halfpenny in the summer, nor less than one ale quart for a halfpenny in the winter, always hot from the kine, as the same was milded and strained. One Trolop, and afterwards Goodman, were farmers there, and had thirty or forty kine to the pail.'

Goodman's Fields, as it became known (the streets covering Goodman's Fields today are Leman Street, Mansell Street and Prescott Street), was later used as tenter ground for cloth-workers, as a fun-fair, and as a drill-yard for volunteers. Always it was in the centre of the action. Thus in 1761 there was a riot outside the Wells Chapel when Mr Bradbury, the preacher, was bruised 'in a cruel manner' and knocked down. The chief trouble-maker was taken to the magistrate in a coach, but the coach was stopped by the mob in Whitechapel Road, and the prisoner rescued. Mr Bradbury, who was also in the coach as the material witness, emerged and was knocked down a second time, and was lucky to escape with his life. A few years later there was the case of the father and brother of a young girl who had eloped to a house of ill-fame (one of many) in Goodman's Fields. The newspaper tells us ambiguously that they 'could not without great difficulty take her away in a coach, to the general satisfaction of a numerous crowd of spectators'.

Another claim to fame is that Goodman's Fields was the scene of David Garrick's first professional appearance on any London stage. There had always been a strong musical and theatrical tradition in the East End, but such was the powerful monopoly exercised by the Drury Lane/Convent Garden managements in the early eighteenth century that any rival theatres which looked like achieving popular success would be closed down after an official enquiry requested by the patent theatres. But if you advertised your entertainment as musical rather than dramatic you were usually clear of the law. So performances of Shakespeare's plays would be presented in the 'interval' of a concert. One of the two Goodman's Fields theatres at this time – the more successful – was the New Wells in Wells Street (now Ensign Street), whose spectacular entertainments including 'rope-dancing, posture masters, singing and dancing' would be transferred each September to Bartholemew Fair.

Close by the New Wells was the Alie Street Theatre, run by the ambitious manager, Giffard. In this small but elegant auditorium plays by Shakespeare, Congreve and Fielding were presented. Garrick, who was stage-struck, had acted for a short season at Ipswich under an assumed name. Giffard was a friend of his and was prepared to back the young man's attempts to avoid the career of a wine merchant which his family had intended for him. A failure at the Alie Street Theatre would be disappointing but not fatal; in any case David Garrick did not intend to fail He chose for his debut the title role in *Richard III* – he was a small man and better suited for this part than for one requiring a more heroic physique. The house was small and initially unenthusiastic. Then:

> When information was brought to Richard, that the Duke of Buckingham was taken, Garrick's look and action, when he pronounced the words: '... off with his head! – So much for Buckingham!' were so significant and important, from his visible enjoyment of the incident, that several loud shouts of approbation proclaimed the triumph of the actor and satisfaction of the audience. The death of Richard was accompanied with the loudest gratulation of applause.

Within a week or two 'Goodman's Fields was full of the splendour of St James's and Grosvenor Square; the coaches of the nobility filled up the space from Temple-Bar to Whitechapel'. For the remainder of the year Garrick appeared to sensational effect in numerous leading roles, receiving a pound a night, until Giffard offered to take him into partnership. But the big two (the Rank and ABC of the eighteenth century), having suffered a sad loss of revenue while society enjoyed the novelty of travelling east for their entertainment, hit back, and Garrick was suborned into starring at Drury Lane while Giffard's theatre reverted to obscurity. Not long afterwards a new theatre in Leman Street was named in honour of Garrick and was obviously a hall of some pretensions for it was described as 'a place where ladies can seat themselves without rats running over them'. The Garrick was burnt down in the nineteenth century, before which, according to Mayhew it had been a favourite haunt of dustmen who 'greatly enjoy the melodramas performed in the second class minor theatres, especially if there be plenty of murdering scenes in them'.

Such places as the Garrick, the East London, the Effingham, the Standard, the City, and the Oriental were rough and ready, but the 'penny gaffs', as they were popularly known, were merely rough. Audiences, who paid a penny for an hour's entertainment, two twenty minute plays with a song between, were young and raucous and threw fish-bones if they felt bored. Naturally the authorities claimed that such places were hot-beds of vice (probably they were) and wished to have them closed down, but the penny gaffs usually stayed within the letter of the law by performing without dialogue such popular pieces as *The Bloodstained Handkerchief*, or *The Murder in the Cottage*.

With the notable exceptions of the Theatre Royal, Stratford East, and the Half Moon, I know of no surviving theatres in the East End.

I had not meant to run ahead of myself in this theatrical manner, but to continue chronologically with a brief history of Whitechapel, and so I shall. Stepney had played host in medieval times to those craftsmen who were not members of livery guilds but could ply their trade outside the city walls. These might be foreigners or they might have disgraced themselves in some way. They included bakers and brewers and particularly butchers, who were traditional elements in Aldgate and Whitechapel until recent years. Says Ralph in Beaumont and Fletcher's play *The Knight of the Burning Pestle*:

> Ancients, let your colours fly, but have a great care of the butchers' hooks
> at Whitechapel; they have been the death of many a fair ancient.

It had been forbidden in 1371 for butchers to slaughter cattle within the city walls, so they slaughtered them in Whitechapel. It was an ill wind which blew along the Essex Road . . . The brewers are still there, and the three great breweries of Truman, Hanbury and Buxton in Brick Lane (founded 1666), Watney Mann in Whitechapel Road (founded 1708) and Charrington's in Mile End (founded 1759) were examples to all ambitious Eastenders that one could always make a fortune from human frailities. One member of the Charrington family had other priorities. Frederick Charrington, who burned a bundle of bank notes when he was nine, witnessed a brutal scene outside a tavern eleven years later in which a drunkard knocked his wife to the ground when she pleaded to him for money to buy bread for the children. Above the door of the pub a familiar name could be seen:

> It suddenly flashed into my mind [wrote Frederick] that that was only one
> case of dreadful misery and fiendish brutality in one of the several hundred
> public houses our firm possessed . . . What a frightful responsibility for evil
> rested upon us.

Converted to temperance, he became a tireless campaigner for sobriety, opening the vast Great Assembly Hall in Mile End Road in 1886. Disliking sex as much as drink, DOYK (Down On Your Knees) Charrington turned his fervent attention to brothels, inviting the girls to breakfast and plying them with ham and beef and coffee and 'Auld Land Syne' on the organ. According to a biographer: 'The blackest scoundrels in London . . . hid themselves like frightened birds at the mere rumour of his approach'.

Besides the bakeries, the butcheries, the breweries, the bars and the brothels, Whitechapel acquired a notable and rather more dignified

Mears and Stainbanks Bell Foundry.

claim to fame, the Bell Foundry. I wonder if this could be the oldest established business in Britain? Mears and Stainbanks bell foundry was established in 1420 at Aldgate. In 1570 – some say 1567 – it moved to the High Street, before moving to its handsome premises on the south of the main road in 1738. Scarcely a bell worthy of the name has been struck anywhere other than at Whitechapel, whence emanated the Bow Bells of St Mary-le-Bow, St Paul's Great Tom, Big Ben (of course), the cathedral bells of Canterbury, Lichfield, Durham and Winchester, a peal of ten at York Minster, Philadelphia's Liberty Bell, and bells for churches from St Petersburg to South Carolina. The tradition was strong in Whitechapel. In 1824 at St Mary's eight heroes rang a complete Peal of Triples on Steadman's principle, no less than 5040 changes in just two hours and fifty-eight minutes (though it may have seemed longer to local residents). One family, the Olivers, have been connected with the manufacture of musical handbells at the foundry for considerably more than two centuries.

Whitechapel had several other landmarks of significance; a windmill used for grinding corn, near St Mary's; the London Hospital; and The Mount, raised in 1642 and levelled in 1806. The Mount was just what it sounds like. It was no less than 329 feet long by 182 feet wide, about the height of a church plus steeple, and surrounded by a trench. Most historians agree that its original purpose was to defend the City of London after the Battle of Edge Hill against the Royalist Cavalry. There was a rumour that it was used as a communal burial pit for victims of the Great Plague, and that debris from the Fire of London was piled on top of what became a glorified builder's skip. Of course it was only a part of London's defences, which consisted of entrenchments and forts as well as earthworks, and the people of London manned these defences enthusiastically. I quote from a contemporary newspaper:

> On the 23rd of May three thousand porters went voluntarily to the works with their wives and children; on the 5th of June five thousand shoemakers worked in the trenches: on the 7th six thousand tailors; on the 9th of June five thousand sailors and persons connected with the river laboured in the Mile-End and Shadwell works. It was on this day that Sir Kenelm Digby, while standing on the Mount, was arrested as a spy and conveyed a prisoner to Winchester House.

When the Mount was levelled it was feared that the dead bodies of plague victims would create a serious hazard to health. More sinister were those who hoped to find articles of value among the corpses and the debris of the fire. But in the event nobody's health suffered and nobody was made any the richer. Today Mount Terrace and East Mount Street either side of the Hospital mark the site of this man-made excrescence.

Like the Bell Foundry the London Hospital was, and is, a landmark much beloved of Eastenders. It was founded in 1740 as a refuge for sick seamen, watermen and dock labourers, and expanded both in size and in efficiency until it became the largest hospital in England. Alcoholism, cholera and flu sent many patients there, and amongst its most famous doctors was one Barnardo, who in 1866 witnessed sixteen cholera deaths in the hospital within a single day. The doctor had intended to become a medical missionary in China, but the plight of the homeless children in Whitechapel could not, he found, be ignored. In his attempts to raise patrons he invited Lord Shaftesbury to come and see what conditions were like in the East End. In Billingsgate Fish Market, Barnardo showed Shaftesbury a tarpaulin concealing a pile of wooden crates. From under the tarpaulin seventy-three ragged children emerged, verminous and pitiful. 'All London shall know of this!' cried Shaftesbury, and very soon it did. Barnardo's slogan was 'No destitute boy ever turned away', and although his philanthropic career was accompanied by numerous scandals and ill-motivated gossip, there is no doubt that such men as

The London Hospital.

Barnardo, General Booth, Frederick Charrington and the others, did a vast amount to ease the desperate conditions of life suffered by so many people, innocent, inadequate, and incompetent, in the slums of Whitechapel.

Perhaps the most interesting case is that of Canon Barnett and his wife. The Rev. Samuel Augustine Barnett, prosperous, shabby, punctilious and eccentric, had as his parish St Jude's, Whitechapel. It was a rough parish ('perhaps the worst district in London,' said the Bishop, 'containing . . . a large population of Jews and thieves'), the church was squalid and so was the vicarage. Henrietta Barnett wrote:

> When Mr Barnett and I went to see our proposed home, it was market day, and the main street was filled with haycarts, entangled among which were scores of frightened cattle being driven to the slaughter-house. The people were dirty and bedraggled, the children neglected, the beer shops full, the schools shut up. I can recall the realisation of the immensity of our task and the fear of failure to reach or to help those crowds of people, with vice, woe and lawlessness written across their faces.

What was worst of all was that nobody would come to church. Never mind. Samuel and Henrietta organised Sunday Schools, evening classes, home visits, employment, and improved housing. They set up a small bandstand outside the church, but instead of listening to the music, the people danced to it, even, on occasion, rather improperly. When Samuel at once stopped the entertainment, he and Henrietta were stoned. 'And it's us as pays you!' somebody shouted.

Concerned with moral fibre, they organised numerous improving societies such as the Bank of White and Good, and the Guild of Hope and Pity. Henrietta sold her jewellery and bought three brothels, attempting to rehabilitate the girls. Who knows whether the girls were grateful? Every month the couple entertained their parishioners with improving evenings, which did not always improve as the guests grew rowdier and stole the food. In 1881 an exhibition of objects brought back by the Barnetts from Egypt was arranged in three school rooms behind the church. Pictures were also displayed, and – perhaps surprisingly – the event was a success. More than 10,000 people paid threepence each to visit the show. After the first season the admission charge was abolished, never to be reimposed, and the Gallery (though perhaps too modest to merit the name) became established with 60,000 visitors during twelve days in March 1886 (of course the exhibitions could only be held during the school holidays). Samuel was colour blind and regretted that all pictures could not be ethical allegories, such as his favourite 'Time, Death and Judgement' by Watts, but Henrietta, 'as sentient as he was idealistic' advised him on aesthetic matters with a bias in favour of de Morgan's pottery and William Morris's designs.

There were many problems. The Barnetts kept the exhibitions open on Sundays, for that was the day when working people were freest to go. The Lord's Day Observance Society picketed, and threatened visitors with eternal damnation. The Bishops also brought pressure to bear on the vicar of St Jude's. But the motto of the Whitechapel Art movement was staunch and proud. It was taken from Ruskin: 'Life without work is guilt and work without art is brutality.'

Less fashionably, Barnett was used to proclaim that what he wanted to supply was 'the highest art for the lowest people'.

There were problems of a more technical nature too. Mrs Barnett wrote:

> The people crowded and lingered around a picture with a story and, as the floors were weak, only one popular canvas could be placed on each wall. Also the means of entrance and exit were small, visitors sometimes drunken, and panic easily aroused in crowds.

Eventually, after many false alarms and much heartbreak, a permanent home was set up with an adequate endowment scheme. Thus was opened on 14 March 1901 the Whitechapel Art Gallery, whose terracotta art nouveau frontage and airy, spacious interior became so

Whitechapel Art Gallery

familiar to aesthetes from the West End and, rather less frequently, Whitechapel folk. By a sad irony the Barnetts could not attend the opening of their fantasy made reality (crimson hessian walls and Lord Rosebery as Guest of Honour), for they were mourning the death of their adopted daughter. Not long afterwards Barnett was appointed Canon and Sub-Dean of Westminster Abbey.

Recently, with marvellous photographic exhibitions of East-End life, the gallery has become more genuinely 'popular', and it has just concluded an ambitious extension scheme with a lecture theatre, a library and goodness knows what. The site of the old library is precisely where the celebrated hay market used to be held, and in its foyer next door to

The mosaic of the 1788 Hay Fair.

the gallery is a delightful mosaic of that event in 1788. Notice not only the amorous predilictions of the two young men and the merchant in the purple hat, but also the intriguing detail that the horses are wearing ear-muffs.

The library is wonderful, and has been a great bringer-on of tragic geniuses, such as Isaac Rosenberg, the poet, and Mark Gertler, the artist – brilliant, doomed youths. This is what Jacob Bronowski, scientist, had to say about the Whitechapel Library, in his inaugural address as president of the Library Association:

As a boy of twelve, newly come to this country, and speaking only a few words of English, I was taken by another boy to see the Librarian at the Public Library in Whitechapel . . . I remember the thin, elderly man with spectacles and a moustache whom I asked for help. I wanted a book which

I could read with pleasure, which I could follow, and from which I could learn good English. I do not know whether the librarian entirely grasped these broken demands, which sound so easy and are so difficult to meet. Whether he did or did not, he gave me Mr Midshipman Easy. I have considered it the perfect choice ever since.

The Gallery and Library were hugely significant, but they only form a part of Barnett's legacy to Whitechapel. He it was who was responsible for the Artisans Dwelling Act which made it possible to condemn dwellings regarded as unfit for human habitation, for the Sanitation Act which ensured that sewers were connected, and for the Children's Holiday Fund. Most substantial of all though was his influence in creating 'the university of the slums', Toynbee Hall.

This originated with a young Oxford student called Denison who was so affected by the gulf between the rich and the poor in the east end of London that in 1867 he took lodgings near the London Hospital to experience at first hand what life was like for the Whitechapel poor. Others from Oxford and Cambridge followed Denison's example, and by 1874 quite a few students, usually graduates, would share in the parish work of Barnett's church, St Jude's. Notable amongst the group, who were *not* impelled, like most of the East-End reformers, by evangelical Christian zeal, were Arnold Toynbee, Sidney Ball, A. L. Smith and Arthur Sidgwick. Thus in 1884 was born the first of the East-End settlements, and it was named after the philosopher and economist Toynbee, who was to die before the Hall, a derelict school in Commercial Street, had opened. At Toynbee Hall, Mrs Sidney Webb worked on 'Sweating in East London' and Charles Booth did the research which produced his massive volume The Life and labour of London. Here Shaw debated and Ben Tillet, Tom Mann and John Burns of the Social Democratic Federation (an early version of the Labour Party) organised the dockers. Here too Basil Henriques worked before setting up the most celebrated of the Jewish Settlements, the Oxford and St George's, in which I lived for a few months after leaving university. That was in Berners Street, now called Henriques Street after Sir Basil, Magistrate, enthusiast, controversialist and writer.

With so many reformers at work, so many shelters and missions and institutes and clubs, one might have expected Whitechapel to bloom into the new Jerusalem, but there were sinister forces doing the devil's work too. And yet it seems that Jack the Ripper was inspired to his dirty work by motives not so very different from those of Canon Barnett. At any rate we know that his victims were prostitutes. And ironically his own perverted brand of social reforming gave Whitechapel an identity, a glamour even, that it could not otherwise have acquired. The story has been told too often to warrant re-telling here, or at least the many stories have, for we shall now never know whether the Ripper was the Viennese Jew, Ritler; or the Polish Jew, Pizer; or a soldier from the Tower of London; or a ritual butcher or *shochet;* or an anarchist from the International Workmen's Club; or the Duke of Clarence; or a Russian Secret agent; or a local midwife; or a barrister called Druitt who looked just like the Duke of Clarence; or . . .

There are many clues, but no certainties. The most intriguing clue is the letter to the Central News Agency (the third in the series) in which the killer uses his notorious nickname – if indeed the letter came from the killer. It reads:

I'm not a butcher,
I'm not a Yid,
Nor yet a foreign skipper,
But I'm your own high-hearted friend,
Yours truly,
Jack the Ripper.

Tours of Jack the Ripper country, the courts and alleyways in which the slaughterings and disembowellings took place, are regular tourist attractions in Whitehall. It really is strange what you have to do to become a household name. If you wish to study the case seriously you should read *Encyclopaedia of Murder* by Colin Wilson and Pat Pitman (1964) or *Jack the Ripper* by David Farson (1972).

Whitechapel is the home too of Bloom's, the doyen of kosher restaurants. Morris Bloom opened his first restaurant in Brick Lane in 1920 and, his talents appreciated by immigrants nostalgic for gedempte meatballs and lockshen, for stuffed kishka and kneidlach, never looked back. Within ten years he had opened a kosher food factory, and in 1960 his son, Sidney, inaugurated a canning department so that Bloom's food, supervised by a rabbi and a religious adviser every day, may be eaten nationwide. The two London branches (90 Whitechapel High Street, E1 and 130 Golders Green Road, NW11) serve predictable and hugely sustaining food which may either be eaten at a table (slow) or directly from the serving counter, which is a great place to eavesdrop.

Petticoat Lane you will find on the maps as Middlesex Street, being the old boundary between the City of London and the County of Middlesex. It used to be called Hog's Lane. Here it still says 'George Davis is innocent' on the walls, but an Irishman shouts 'The Wages of Sin are Death!' to bemused-looking Muslims at the south end of the Lane. The stalls in Petticoat Lane were once the prerogative of the Irish, then the Jews took it over – 'We are perhaps the sons of dealers in old clothes, but we are the grandsons of prophets' – and now it is principally Moslem territory.

But the traders are true cockneys. 'Everything guaranteed knocked off!' cries one. 'Yesterday evening this watch was in the window of a jeweller's shop in Wolverhampton!' cries another. And 'straight off the back of a lorry!' cries the third. The philosophy of the Lane has always been and remains 'To sell something you have to someone who wants it – that is not business. But to sell something you don't have to someone who doesn't want it – *that* is business.'

Don't think you'll find antiques there. You'll find: 'Myers: the oldest eel stall in England', but that doesn't make the eels antique. And you may still find pub mirrors, and knickers embroidered: 'Tested and approved. Signed Ivor Biggun' and a pearly king collecting for the handicapped, but not antiques. Last time I was there I could have bought dolly pegs and bowler hats and a jar of fifty-four wizard lollipops and silk scarves and screwdrivers and a small carboard box which, when you pull the string, clucks like a chicken. Probably the only thing you won't find in Petticoat Lane is petticoats, but then it is an imperfect world and improving very slowly. One thing remains as true now as it was when the admirable Henry Mayhew conducted his exhaustive survey into London life. I quote:

> Another peculiarity pertaining alike to this shop and street locality is, that everything is at the veriest minimum of price; though it may not be asked, it will assuredly be taken. The bottle of lemonade which is elsewhere a penny is here a halfpenny. . .' [and he goes into fascinating detail at too great a length to quote here].

For the local people in past centuries and again today, the most important market is not Petticoat Lane, (though that may bring gawping tourists to the region), but the stalls in the Whitechapel Road which run from the point where the road widens, just beyond the old churchyard of St Mary Matfelon, to the Trinity Almshouses built by Wren 'for the Commanders of Ships or the Widoes of such 1698'. Walter Besant described how it used to be:

> Here are displayed all kinds of things; bits of secondhand furniture, such as the head of a wooden bed . . . skates sold cheap in summer, light clothing in winter; workmen's tools of every kind . . . books, boots, shoes . . . cutlery, hats and caps; rat-traps and mouse-traps and bird-cages; flowers and seeds; skittles . . . bloaters and haddocks . . .

These days the emphasis is on household goods, but there is no question that the true function of the market is social. Leave convenience shopping to the supermarkets; this is where humanity survives.

Whitechapel Road (together with Mile End Road, Aldgate and Whitechapel High Street) comprises the spine of the East End. John Strype described it as: 'a great thoroughfare, being the Essex Road and well resorted unto, and accommodated with good inns for the reception of travellers, and for horses, carts, coaches and wagons'. In the old days, there was the hay market, the boxing booths, the penny gaffs, the bell foundry, the market, the alms houses, the People's Palace, the Library and Whitechapel Art Gallery, the Yiddish theatre, the Mount, the Hospital and Jack the Ripper. There was the Hoop and Grapes (at 46 Aldgate High St), a pub in London's oldest licensed premises, standing on cellars that go back to the thirteenth century. The cellars were remarkable too for the 'lug-hole' at which the landlord could hear what his customers were saying about the beer. This timber-framed building, which survived the Great Fire by a mere fifty yards, is unequalled in London and has now been converted into offices, having been (like so much that is worth preserving) under imminent threat of demolition. There were the breweries and the bakers and the butchers and the popular sport of releasing a maddened ox or bullock into the crowded streets. (This resulted in a dreadful tragedy in 1815 when an infuriated bullock attacked a five-year-old boy opposite the London Hospital and, goring him in the mouth, killed him instantly. The crowd continued to bait the beast which killed an old lady nearby before being secured.) There were frequent terrible fires, the worst of which took place in the sugar-warehouses and the sweat-shops, which fires produced a romantic folk-hero in the quadruped shape of Bill, a terrier belonging to a Mr Wood, fire escape conductor of 6 Silk Street, Cripplegate. Bill had an unerring nose for a fire. Having sniffed one out he would bark until his master arrived with the fire-cart. Then he would investigate the burning building (having his coat scalded off on occasion) and loudly draw attention to any inhabitants. At the age of six he was presented by Whitechapel parishioners with a chased silver collar, for having saved no fewer than seventy-two lives.

There was Sidney Street, made famous by Peter the Painter, and there were slums, prostitution and degradation of all kinds. Now there is a new style. Gardiner's clothing store, outfitters of so many sailors, has gone, and many of the old buildings that were, in truth, not really worth preserving. Incongruous new developments – a boisterous new leisure centre (Sedgwick House), and a chocolate-box mosque next to the Fiat agents – burgeon and sprout amidst the Victorian pubs and the Alis and Ahmeds of the fashion wholesalers.

Whitechapel is, and was, a trading post. But will it remain so? Now that the docks have outlived their usefulness, new generations of hungry immigrants may settle around Heathrow, Stanstead, or Gatwick. Well no, the docks have *not* outlived their usefulness; they are to be (if you believe the developers) the new Jerusalem, golden in the sunshine. And then Whitechapel will be given back to – perhaps – the butchers, the bakers and the brewers.

5

Borough High Street
The first suburb

St George's Fields are fields no more,
The trowel supersedes the plough;
Swamps huge an inundate of yore,
Are changed to civic villas now . . .

– The Spread of London (1813)

Chaucer's pilgrims set off from the Tabard Inn. Dickens's father was incarcerated in the Marshalsea prison for debtors. Chaucer's friend, the poet John Gower, is in Southwark Cathedral, and there are memorials to John Fletcher and Philip Massinger, dramatists, as well as to Shakespeare. Shakespeare's theatre was close by and his unfortunate brother (who died of the plague) is buried in Southwark Cathedral. Keats was a student at Guy's hospital, and Dr Johnson was a frequent visitor to Mrs Thrale's house; her father Henry owned the Barclay and Perkins brewery nearby. At the Thrale's house in Park Street, Hester held a literary salon, and entertained, among many others, Oliver Goldsmith, who had a doctor's practice on Bankside. John Harvard, who founded an educational establishment somewhere in America, was born in the Borough and baptised in Southwark Cathedral (then St Saviour's church). As you have gathered, the area is so rich with literary ghosts that the gutters run with ink and the stallholders in Borough Market speak in blank verse. Well, almost.

Southwark, Bankside, and the Borough are more or less interchangeable names for the area which forms a T, with the upright Borough High Street, and the crossbar the south bank of the Thames from St Mary Overies Wharf to Tooley Street. Southwark, built on marshes, was London's first suburb. There, approaching London Bridge along Watling Street from Dover and the South-Coast ports, the Romans would rest and refresh themselves. In 1014 the Danes, having occupied the city and fortified Southwark (literally the south works), defended London Bridge against King Ethelred of England and King Olaf of Norway, who cunningly pulled down the struts of the bridge by attaching ropes to them

Left: Borough Market and Southwark Cathedral.

and rowing energetically downstream. (Tooley Street is a corruption of St Olave's Street, and a church named after Olaf stood more or less where the Magistrates' Court stands today.)

King Harold crossed the Bridge to meet William the Conqueror, but all to no avail. The Normans burned down Southwark. Wisely the next and most famous London Bridge was built (by Peter de Colechurch, Bridgemaster) of stone, with nineteen narrow arches, and for some 550 years it remained the only bridge over the Thames. On it were shops, houses, a chapel, and a large gate at the Southwark end. On St George's day 1390 a tournament was held on the bridge, a test of courage between Lord Wells, Richard II's ambassador in Scotland, and Sir David Lindsay, Earl of Crawford. The King presided and had guaranteed Sir David safe conduct with his entourage. So still did the Scotsman sit in his saddle despite the vehement impulse of the charge and the thrust of the lances that spectators accused him of being tied to it. Sir David was no cheat, and leapt off his charger at once, vaulting back into the saddle without assistance. When inevitably Lord Wells was unhorsed, Sir David embraced him tenderly until he revived. For three months Lindsay remained in England, but on his returning home the brave Scotsman founded a chantry at Dundee, providing £32 for 'seven priests and divers virgins' to sing anthems to St George. On top of the Bridge the heads of criminals used to be exposed, and not that long before the great tourney Sir William Wallace's noble head had been one of them. No wonder Sir David was inspired to such feats of chivalry.

Across the Bridge (and along Borough High Street) passed the Black Prince, returning from Poitiers with the captive King John of France, and Henry V in triumph after Agincourt; also Margaret of Anjou to marry Henry VI, Katherine of Aragon to marry Prince Arthur. And, of course, the Canterbury pilgrims. Under it was practised the dangerous and enterprising sport of 'shooting the bridge'. 'London Bridge', says the old proverb, 'is for wise men to go over and fools to go under.'

Also, to the South of the bridge was the church, upon whose site was to be built the gothic cathedral. This was St Mary Overie, and I would be cheating if I did not pass on to you the romantic story attaching to its name. (More prosaic historians believe that 'Overie' meant 'over the river' but I don't.)

Mary was the daughter of Overs, the ferryman who carried travellers across the river long before the bridge was built. Her father was miserly beyond belief, and to cut down on household expenses he pretended to be dead, fancying that all those around him would go into mourning, and for a while eat rather less than they were accustomed to. How wrong can one be! No sooner was his death recorded than a great feast was prepared. The infuriated ferryman at once came to life again, but was taken to be a ghost by a boatman, who struck the ferryman on the head with an oar, killing him instantly. Mary then sent for her lover who lived out of town and of whom the ferryman had thoroughly disapproved. In the urgency of his passion, the young man spurred on his horse over-ambitiously, he fell off and died. Mary, later and rather improbably canonised as St Mary, responded to these successive disasters by building a nunnery with the profits of the ferry, and entering it herself, though whether as noviciate or as mother superior I'm afraid I can't tell you.

Whether the story be mythical or true, we do know that there had been a nunnery there, and that it was dissolved by St Swithin, the Bishop of Winchester, who set up a college of secular priests on the site. After the Norman Conquest the college or monasterium passed to Odo, Bishop of Bayeux, and afterwards to William de Warenne, the Earl of Surrey. A new church was built in 1106, and this inherited the name St Mary Overie. Here the 'Black Canons' of St Augustine served, building a priory nearby. Simultaneously the Bishops of Winchester, whose diocese stretched as far as London Bridge, were building themselves a Palace, known as Winchester House. Famous residents included William of Wykeham, founder of Winchester School, and Lancelot Andrewes, whose resplendent tomb enhances the Cathedral. Lancelot Andrewes is a true saint. Besides his scholarly life and unselfish works, he was partly responsible for the Authorised Version of the Bible, which less scholarly and less saintly Christians recently betrayed into 'modern' English. A fragment of Winchester House (or Winchester Palace) remains – just a part of the west wall and a very lovely rose window still stands in Clink Street. Clink Street? Well yes. The original 'Clink' was the Bishops' own prison, in which those who offended against justice within the Bishops' own manor were confined. It was an underground dungeon lying squelchily between the pike gardens and the sewers.

A severe punishment for 'such as should brabble or frey, or break the peace on the Bank' (John Stow, 1598). There was a lot of breaking the peace, because not too far from the elegance of the Bishops' residence was 'the Bordello or Stewes, a place so called, of certaine stew housaes privileged there, for the repaire of incontinent men to the like women'. Most scolds, or quarrelsome women, were sentenced to the ducking stool, a lot worse than it sounds, for they were ducked into the sewer at Bank End. Cases which were regarded as more serious would be tried by the all-male jurors of the court leet within the Liberty of the Clink. One of the most serious crimes was heresy, and many eminent heretics of all persuasions were confined to the Clink. When Queen Mary was on the throne, Protestants would be tried in St Mary's, incarcerated in the Clink, and taken over the bridge to be burnt at Smithfield. Under Elizabeth, Catholics eked out a dark and pestilential existence underground. A vivid picture of the squalour of the Clink may be observed within the London Dungeons, a gruesome tourist attraction specialising in not altogether convincing displays of eviscerations, amputations, mutilations and mutations. A pleasanter reminder of the Clink are the many bollards scattered around Bankside and the Borough Market. Purchased from the local iron and nail warehouse, many are inscribed 'Clink 1812'. Clink in this context refers to the Commissioner for Clink Pavements, because the Clink itself was finally obliterated in 1780.

There had been other notorious prisons in Southwark, namely the Marshalsea, the King's Bench, the Borough Compter, and the White Lion or County Gaol. The Marshalsea is best known, of course, from Dickens. Here young Charles, staying in Lant Street, visited his father between 1823 and 1824, and here the Dorrit family could be found, but John Wesley's view of the place in 1753 is the most vivid:

> Oh shame to man that there should be such a place, such a picture of hell upon earth! And shame to those who bear the name of Christ that there should need any prison at all in Christendom! In the afternoon I visited many of the sick; but such scenes, who could see unmoved?

Adjoining the Marshalsea was another prison, the King's Bench. The site of both runs (according to the plaques) from the Tiling and Roofing Centre at Chapel Court to St George's Gardens. Held in the King's Bench, besides Mr Micawber waiting for something to turn up, were many eminent debtors, including John Wilkes (actually put away for libel not debt); Tobias Smollett; and Haydon, who painted 'The Mock Election' here. The King's Bench was burned during the Gordon Riots (1780) and was closed eighty years later when imprisonment was no longer – I am delighted to say – regarded as a suitable punishment for debt. A century or so later credit cards were introduced. In fact, the King's Bench had become the most popular debtors' prison in the country. Within the 50-foot-high brick wall there were pumps giving pure spring water, a coffee-house, shops and pubs. It was even possible, for a consideration, to live outside the walls within a prescribed three-mile circumference.

But I had not quite concluded the history of London Bridge (it's a substantial history with several learned tomes on that subject alone). Peter de Colechurch's nineteen-arched bridge, which stood for so long, was replaced (1824-27) by John Rennie's handsome five-arched bridge at the astonishing cost of some two million pounds. While the old bridge had been a mere forty foot wide, this one was still too narrow for the immense load of traffic it had to bear.

In his *London Guide* of 1879 Dickens wrote:

> In order to facilitate traffic, police constables are stationed along the middle of the roadway, and all vehicles travelling at a walking pace only are compelled to keep close to the curb. There are still, however, frequent

blocks, and the bridge should be avoided as much as possible, especially between 9 and 10 a.m. and 4 and 6 p.m.

He adds that, seen from the river, 'it is the handsomest bridge in London'. Well now it is the handsomest bridge in Lake Hayasu City, Arizona, which is where it has been re-erected, and, by a tragic irony, its replacement (one hundred and five foot wide with a central span of three hundred and forty feet, designed some fifteen years ago by Harold K. King) is still clogged with traffic between 9 and 10 a.m. and 4 and 6 p.m., though while you sit and wait for your engine to overheat you have a splendid view (going north) of reflecting glass and Portland stone, leading the eye to the Guardian Royal Exchange building, like a secular Montparnasse. And a splendid view (going south) of the tower of the Cathedral rising proudly, like the tower of the parish church it once was, behind the railway lines. And a splendid view, travelling in either direction, of the river and its banks. For those who claim that the beauty of London has been desecrated, is being desecrated and will continue to be desecrated, it may be salutary to refer to how Nathaniel Hawthorne saw the Bankside at the height of the industrial revolution:

> It seems, indeed, as if the heart of London had been cleft open for the mere purpose of showing how rotten annd drearily mean it had become. The shore is lined with the shabbiest, blackest, and ugliest buildings that can be imagined, decayed workhouses with blind windows, and wharves that look ruinous; insomuch that, had I known nothing more of the world's metropolis, I might have fancied that it had already experienced the downfall which I have heard commercial and financial prophets predict for it, within the century. And the muddy tide of the Thames, reflecting nothing, and hiding a million of unclean streets within its breast, – a sort of guilty conscience, as it were, unwholesome with the rivulets of sin that constantly flow into it, – is just the dismal stream to glide by such a city.

That was 1870, but if we look back to 1549 we find in the court leet books for Southwark the following typical entry:

> Presentid that certaine persons doo not onlye there easements in fowle lane but cast chamber pottes which is a greate anyaunce to the people that waye passinge wherefor yt is pained to amend the same by Candlemas next uppon paine of every tyme soe offending xxd.

Part of the problem was that the market was on the banks of the river. Butchers were required to throw entrails into the river only at night when the river was in a flood and after the guts had been chopped up so that they were no more than a yard long.

These days, of course, the Thames sparkles with purity and a casual glance upstream from London Bridge gives little sense of the gloomy landscape recorded by Hawthorne. A stroll along Borough High Street, indeed, gives every indication of a flourishing commercial centre. There are lawyers and accountants and wholesalers and builders. The modern office developments are varied and tactfully ugly. Much care has been taken over horizontal jambs and such, but the effect is depressing. Borough High Street was chiefly famous, of course, for its hop warehouses, its coaching inns, and Barclay and Perkins brewery. The hop warehouses are commemorated in a splendid carved adornment commandingly sited above the High Street: 'W. H. and H. le May – Hop Factors'. There is a decoration of hop plants too on the ornate iron gates to Central Buildings in Southwark Street, for this was the Hop and Malt Exchange, the very heart of the hop industry of Kent. Southwark beer has a long and distinguished history from Chaucerian England – the Miller in the Canterbury Tales apologises in advance lest his words become muddled and blames it on too much Southwark Ale – down to 1982 when Courage closed its two local breweries. Which reminds me that when Mr Thrale's premises were being sold Dr Johnson could be seen bustling about with an ink-horn and pen in his button-hole like an exciseman. 'We are not here to sell a parcel of vats and boilers', he remarked, 'but the potentiality of growing rich beyond the dreams of avarice.'

Of all the inns which rubbed shoulders along Borough High Street, and many of which are commemorated in the names of the courtyards which still bristle on either side of the thoroughfare, the most famous is the George. It is the only one to have survived. Gone are the Tabard, the Queen's Head, the Catherine Wheel, the Three Tuns, the Grapes, the Spur, the White Hart, the Pope's Head and a host of others. The King's Arms is still there, in Newcomen Street, but the only old thing about it is the magnificently sculptured royal coat of arms dated 1760, and this was removed from the South Gate of London Bridge. The White Hart was the headquarters for Jack Cade's rebellion of 1450. Remember *Henry VI* when Shakespeare has the rebel ask:

> Will you needs be hanged with your pardons about your necks? Hath my sword therefore broken through London gates that you should leave me at the 'White Hart' in Southwark?

Burned down in the Southwark fire, ten years after the Great Fire of London and almost as destructive, the White Hart was rebuilt and became the rendezvous for Jingle and Rachael Wardle, as well as Sam Weller's place of employment. When I say that the George has survived I am exaggerating slightly, for only a part of it has survived, the north and east sides having been demolished by a railway company. But the galleried remaining south-side deserves more than a cursory mention

The George, Borough High Street.

since it is possibly the oldest, and almost certainly the most celebrated pub in the world. Like the White Hart and the Elephant, the George, which was only five hundred yards from Shakespear's Globe Theatre, is mentioned by Will, who refers in *King John* to: 'St George, that swing'd the dragon, and e'er since sits on his horseback at mine hostess' day,' but the St George and Dragon (it lost the 'St' after the reformation and lost the dragon somewhere along the way) had been a popular inn for at least two hundred and fifty years before Shakespeare drank sack there. In Borough High Street alone there were twenty-three coaching inns, and from each yard a coach would leave for a different destination; a bit like the Victoria Coach Station. Most of these inns could comfortably accommodate two hundred travellers, and feed them, and entertain them with music and dancing and plays (as are still occasionally performed at the George). During the seventeenth century the failure of the Royal Mint to produce enough coins resulted in the George issuing its own coinage, and it was one establishment at which, remarkably in those days, you could count on sleeping between clean sheets. (This concern for its lodgers survived until the present century. When that inveterate traveller, H. V. Morton, fulfilled a life-long ambition and spent a night sleeping in a four-poster at the George, he discovered after breakfast that the chambermaid had darned two pairs of his socks.) Although it frequently changed hands the George was always popular and profitable. In the early nineteenth century there are account books to show that a quarterloaf which cost ninepence and sixpennyworth of butter could be relied upon to produce thirteen rounds of toast at threepence a round. The George was popular with secret and sometimes cranky clubs. (It still is. On a recent visit I found the main dining room full of Rotarians.) The Four O'Clockers met there, and so did the Old Chums, the most secret Brotherhood of the Rolling Stones, and the Twelve Club, whose twelve members were all buyers in West End stores.

In the early part of the present century Agnes Murray, the licensee, was given a parrot. Not just a parrot but a copper-bottomed money-back guarantee that the bird would have learned to talk within three months. But it didn't. Nor did Agnes choose to demand a replacement. 'This parrot has brought good business to the George,' she said. 'Every man who thinks he can make a parrot talk comes here to have a try . . . None of them can, but they talk to their friends and relatives about him. So the parrot who cannot talk is the talk of the town.'

The George was donated by the Great Northern Railway company to the National Trust in 1937, and it was leased first to Flowers, and now to Whitbreads. Interrupted by what sound ominously like 'improvements', the George does not currently present Shakespeare productions in the yard, but it will again when the construction work, including 'a picturesque Victorian gallery of shops', is completed. Already the George bears all the signs of a tourist attraction, i.e. no salt in the vegetables and a signpost saying Restaurant which points straight towards the lavatories.

The inn is haunted, of course, by suitably Elizabethan and Victorian ghosts which tap on the walls, lock the doors, and behave in the footling ways of conventional ghosts.

Despite the market and the beer and the coaching inns and the prisons and the stews, Southwark was by no means a cultural desert, even after the four bankside theatres (The Rose, The Swan, The Hope and The Globe) closed down. There was the Southwark School of Glaziers in the sixteenth century, men called Barnard Flower and Galyon Hone and Peter Nicholson, who received the accolade of the royal warrant and

gave us, amongst lesser glories, the glowing windows of King's College
Chapel in Cambridge. There were the Southwark printers who gave us
the Coverdale Bible (and recently Letts Diaries). There were sculptors –
often Dutchmen – and potters, who specialised in the delightful tin-
glazed earthenware known as delftware. The craftsmen and artists who
set up their pottery kilns at Liverpool, at Bristol and in Lambeth, all
came from Southwark. There were Huguenot weavers here, as in Whitechapel, and the Apsley Pellatts cutting their colourful glass artefacts at
the Falcon Glassworks during the nineteenth century. And in the
twentieth music bursts from Southwark Cathedral at lunchtime (organ
on Mondays, chamber music on Tuesdays, recorded music on Thursdays
– all at 1.15 p.m.) consoling the meths drinkers in the garden and
encouraging the lovers entwined on the grass to name the day. The
organ, which is publicly exercised on Mondays, is rather a special one,
the finest achievement of the great T. C. Lewis, and the only Lewis organ
which remains to us in anything like its original condition. (Donations
for essential work on the console to the Organ Appeal, 9a St Thomas
Street, SE1 will be gratefully received.) There is much else to be enjoyed
in the Cathedral, where I once spent an astonishing evening with Edith
Evans and Edna O'Brien, which I would tell you about if I were less
discreet. The glory of the place, to my eye, is the retro-choir with its fan
tracery the colour of Carrara marble, so that you feel you are standing in a
copse of silver birches. Mind you, the Harvard Chapel, simple and
dignified, is a worthy tribute to a great philanthropist, who is also
commemorated in the High Street by the John Harvard library of local
history. John Harvard's father was churchwarden at Southwark Cathedral when it was just St Saviours Church. For the less spiritual, the
Cathedral has much to offer by way of curiosities. There's a monument to
Lionel Lockyer, a physician whose stone corpse still has a slightly
cunning look, although the eyes are shut. Says the legend:

> His Virtues and his Pills are so well known
> That Envy can't confine them under Stone.
> But they'll survive his dust and not expire
> Till all things else at th' Universal Fire.

You might also find an epitaph to a Mr Garrard, a local grocer:

> Weep not for him, since he is gone before
> To Heaven, where Grocers there are many more.

But what is *special* about Southwark Cathedral is not so much its
literary associations, its history, its organ, its tombs, or even its retro-
choir, but *where* it is. What other Cathedral is cheek by jowl with a
vegetable market, overlooked by an antique railway line, and hurried
past daily by myriads of worried commuters, enjoying a breath of fresh air

between the crowded train and the over-heated office? A fine contemporary development, Minerva House, is thrusting itself between the Cathedral and the river.

Satisfactorily, Borough High Street may be thought of as linking the comforting tower, so reminiscent of a parish church, of the Cathedral with the elegant classicism of the spire of St George the Martyr (by John Price 1733–36, restored in 1952 after bomb damage), the spire standing on an eight-sided tower. Known, for obvious reasons, as Little Dorrit's Church, it is the resting place of many debtors from the Marshalsea and the King's Bench prisons. In its parish register is an entry: '1610. Michael Banks, executed: did revive again, was in the vestry three hours, and was then carried back and executed again.' Also curious is the clock on the tower. Three dials are illuminated, but the dial facing Bermondsey is not. This is, they say, because the local people of Bermondsey subscribed so meanly towards the erection of the clock that it was felt they should derive no benefit from it at night.

Guy's Hospital is an intriguing mixture of antiquity and modernity. There are two quadrangles, some railings and a statue or two (one by Scheemakers of the founder, Thomas Guy) to remind us of the original hospital which opened in 1726, two years after Guy died. He was a colourful character, the son of a coal merchant at Horsleydown (originally Whores-Lie-Down!) on the south bank of the Thames opposite the Tower. Born in 1644 or 1645 he made his first fortune (improbably enough) importing Bibles from Holland. Later he became a bookseller in Lombard Street, with a contract from Oxford University to print Bibles himself. From Bibles to Bubbles, for he was one of the few to invest in the South Sea Company and get out at the top of the market. The profits of this were put to good use; he endowed three wards at St Thomas's Hospital, then in St Thomas's Street, next to the Cathedral. But this hospital proving inadequate, he built his own hospital just down the road.

Guy's was savagely blitzed in 1940, and the new buildings were started in 1959, though rather delayed, I expect, by the discovery in the foundations of the remains of a Roman boat. We now have a surgical block (New Guy's House) and the vast Guy's Tower (four hundred and eighty feet high), in which is the hospital, the dental school, the children's hospital, and a school. Several sandwich bars in the High Street cater for nurses and doctors who may be observed discussing rugby football while absent-mindedly dissecting a custard tart.

All that is left of the old St Thomas's Hospital, which moved in 1868 to its present location, is the chapel, now the chapter house of the Cathedral, and the operating theatre (open to the public Mondays, Wednesdays and Friday's, from 12.00 noon to 4.00 p.m.). If this horse-shoe shaped survival seems familiar, that may be because it has formed

St Thomas's Hospital operating theatre.

the model for so many dissection scenes in Burke and Hare movies. (Which reminds me of Hitchcock's definition of the cinema as 'Death by a thousand cuts'.) There is a splendid pedimental doorway, through which the casualty patients were carried and an agreeable terrace of eighteenth century houses, in which lived the Treasurer, Preacher, Steward, Cook, and Butler of the hospital. In my experience there are no butlers in hospitals these days.

At the southern end of the bridge there used to be a hotel at the terminus of the Greenwich line, the first such railway hotel in London. Where the Marylebone Hotel had a cycle track on the roof, the London Bridge Hotel had a romantic ballroom in the sky. Hibernia Chambers (a good name for a romantic heroine in a Victorian novel) is the present building on that site.

There is much more in Borough High Street than hospitals, inns, churches and the cries of ghostly Shakespearean actors, and the ghostly feet of characters from Dickens. More even than interesting old bollards and blood-stained operating theatres. There is, for instance, a whole section of Borough High Street beyond Borough Underground Station, which I propose to write nothing at all about, since it is of very little concern though there is, attached to the station, an endearing and tiny flower shop called Cascade Florists, presided over by a white-headed lady of mature elegance.

But I shall write a word or two about the London Bridge Service Station and Car Wash halfway between the King's Arms and St George the Martyr. This does not stick out like a sore thumb; it sticks out like a suppurating, gangrenous digit on the hand of a cardinal. How *can* the developers be permitted to do such things to us? And I shall also mention the curious vista down Union Street, a splendid amalgam of Victorian warehouse architecture with a huge and emphatic sign at the end of it: HENRY GROSS. And one can scarcely ignore the war memorial on the triangular island at the junction of Southwark Street. A soldier, rifle and bayonet at the ready, crouches and peers towards St George the Martyr. Even in this century there were dragons to be killed.

Above: Borough High Street War Memorial.
Right: '. . . the curious vista down Union Street. . .'